To Auntie Andrea From Callum and Tyler

Forgiveness
THE JOURNEY TO HEALING THE HEART

By Audreia Josephs

FOREWORD

This is an extraordinary story of an extraordinary woman's life.

I first met Audreia at a kindness event in the centre of Birmingham in the UK, and soon after the chance - or, you could say, divine - meeting, she became a coaching client of mine. And it is with hugest dose of humility that I accepted the invitation to write the foreword for her first book. I say 'first' because I know this will be one of many.

I was blown away by Audreia's readiness to jump in and do what it took to begin changing her life for the better. As the saying goes, when the student is ready the teacher appears - or in this case when the coachee is ready the life coach appears.

Audreia's personal and spiritual development journey began way before we entered each other's lives, yet it was very quickly clear (in the first week, in fact) that our work together was to cultivate and facilitate her biggest and deepest transformation to date.

You'll discover as you begin to journey with Audreia through the intricate details and inner workings of her precious yet triumphant life that she carries a certain presence that can only be described as regal - regal with a giant gleaming smile.

And even though she lost most of her crown's gems throughout her turbulent history filled with just as many fallings as risings and as many lows as highs, the crown still sits firmly on her head, though she had totally lost sight of it by the time we met.

This is a not only a story of a little girl, a young lady and a woman. This is a story of a spirit that, had it belonged to another, actually could have been quite broken yet is now stronger and more light-filled than ever, a soul who could have easily given up and taken the easy route of grumpy submission, yet is more sure and empowered than ever before. This is not just a story but also a guide. Use it that way. Use it as an upliftment tool in your own life. Take Audreia's golden examples of forgiveness and gratitude; pleasure in the simple things, like human connection and rekindling a childhood talent of art and creativity; unwavering connection to the divine and above all her strong trust that we are all, always always, always taken care of by the universe.

    Take note of the lack of bitterness, resentment and excuses. Take her determination to show up and embrace this life, its lessons and growth opportunities, with her head held high in grace and a prayer on her lips as a matter of routine. Embrace her capacity to give and love and forgive unconditionally. Those are the skills and abilities we as human beings need to practice more. We need to wipe away and release of our wounds, struggles, heartbreak, disappointments and pain.

    Take note, dear ones, and I encourage you to surrender your own journey as you travel with Audreia through hers because I am sure, certain in fact, that as you close the book at the other end, your life will have already begun to transform in the areas that are as ripe and ready as were in Audreia's life the day she and I met on that November day in Birmingham City.

    This is a story of the kind of woman I can only hope to become as I continue to move towards Audreia's years.

Love & Upliftment,
Maria K.

ENDORSEMENTS

"I first met Audreia at a Mind Body Soul event in Birmingham, and right from that very first meeting she left me in no doubt that she was on a mission. Throughout our journey together, I have watched her step out and let go of all the hurt, anger, frustration and fear that stemmed from the years of abuse beginning when she was just five years old. Now standing in her power with energy, full of the warmth, empathy and compassion that comes from an understanding of others through what she has suffered, she is a true motivational teacher. She inspires others to forgive and to heal through her teaching and the release of her first book. She is proof that peace can be found through forgiveness."

- **Alison Forge,** *Agent for Positive Change, author of 'Pocket Positivity'*

"Audreia is an inspiring, passionate individual whose creative essence is continuing to positively shape the lives of others. Her uplifting enthusiasm brightens every room, whilst her holistic knowledge and wisdom is a profound catalyst for forward-thinking. It is a great privilege to know such a dynamic individual."

- **Geraldine Taylor,** *Author*

DEDICATION

I GIVE THANKS AND PRAISE, TO MY CREATOR. WITHOUT MY CREATOR'S LEADING AND GUIDANCE I WOULD BE NOTHING. I THANK ALL OF MY ANGELS FOR ALL OF THEIR SUPPORT AND ASSISTANCE. I ALSO THANK MY ANCESTORS.

This book is dedicated to: John Haughton.(R.I.P.); Cassilda Clarke.(R.I.P.); Doris Miller (R.I.P.); Urcella Haughton (R.I.P.); Adora Card (R.I.P.); Janet Hare AKA Elaine Saunders (R.I.P); Ivy Drysdale; my sons Stephen, Nathan and Peter, my grandsons Marley and De Vante.

ACKNOWLEDGEMENTS

To my husband Carlwyn Josephs: I thank you for your continued support. Even as I have evolved over the years, from the shallow, broken, uncertain person that I was, you were the first person to let me know that I was beautiful. Even when I did not believe it, you kept on saying it for two years, until it finally got through. Growing up, all I ever heard was that I was a chattah box. When my family said that to me, it was never said with positivity. Now here you were telling me that it was a sign of an enquiring mind. You gave me permission to enjoy being me. I am grateful.

To my parents Rubena and Martan (R.I.P.): Everything happens for a reason. I read a book once that stated that our souls chose our parents. After I had read that, I questioned why I would choose you both. At first that was hard information to digest and absorb. In fact at the early stages, I thought that it was a stupid statement. I am at a different place within myself. My awareness has told me, that in choosing you both, has lead me to a place of pure LOVE & FORGIVENESS. So when all is said and done. I am grateful to you both.

To my uncle John Haughton (R.I.P.): Thank you for being a brave traveler. I am grateful for all you did.

To Janet Maxwell: Growing up with you was a nightmare. You were the biggest BRAT on the planet. As one of your older sisters, I am truly so proud to see the strong and powerful woman that you have evolved into. You have taught me that how you start, does not have to be the person you become. Thank you for the support during giving birth to this book. There were things that I did not want to put in this book due to fear and embarrassment. You encouraged me to 'Talk De Ting'. Thank you so much. Of all the people, no one would have expected me and you to be on this road together.

To Howard Haughton: You have been an unwavering support in my life. Any idea that I have presented to you, you have always told me to go for it. Bro, you are wise beyond your years. And to see how our journey started, we have come far.

To Eugenie (Gen) Haughton: Thank you for being there for me. Here is the seed of the prophecy that you made over my life in 2003.

To James (Jim) Haughton: Even though we did not grow up together, we connect on so many levels. You worked so hard, on trying to keep the family connections together. I am grateful.

To Curline (Renna) Bartley: Thank you for being a wonderful sister. Thank you for encouraging me to share my story.

To Auntie Cutie: For being the voice of reason in the storm, plus for all the years of entertainment.

To every one of my brothers and sisters: I have nothing but love for you all.

To all my nephews and nieces: I have been so blessed to have some of the most amazing people who call me Auntie. I love you all and have learnt so much from some of you. The respect that you have shown me has been overwhelming.

To my step children: Adrian, Arron, Dinaisha and my other set of beautiful grandchildren.

Yvonne Henry, Audrey, Marilyn, Mr. Henry (R.I.P.), and Mrs. Henry; Donavan Drysdale, Auntie Gertie, Jean W, Desna Walker, Brenda, Mrs. Graham and the entire family; Maureen Vernon; the class of 1972 class 1.2; Every friend I ever made at Handsworth New Road School; Miss. Rawlingson; Miss Beer (Taylor); Mrs. Gray; Marcia Anderson; Edris Henry; Mrs. Edwards; Angela Cope; Cleaver A. Walker; Cindy Price; Yvette Taylor; Rosaline Graham; Joy; Carmen Shakes; Katrina Smithen. To all of my cousins: I thank you all for the memories. All the beautiful friends I made at FEDEX Birmingham UK. Maria Karpasitis.: Thank you for appearing at the right time in my life. There are so many names that I am unable to remember, but I want to thank you all for being a part of my life journey.

Jennifer Ward: For the amazing picture of me on the back cover. You have continued to be a constant and reliable friend.

SPECIAL MENTION:

To Ava Eagle Brown, my coach, I salute you: I was challenged to write this book. This young woman stood up to me in a way that no one else has ever stood up to me. She did not waver. She held her ground against all of my excuses. She brought out a part of me that I did not even know existed.

I want to truly thank you for holding my hand in the birthing of this book. You believed in me when I was not sure of myself. You have caused me to surprise myself. Thank you for believing in me.

I would also like to extend my thanks to all of Ava's publishing and editing team.

I SEND YOU ALL LOVE, LIGHT & UPLIFTMENT

Audreia J.

TABLE OF CONTENTS

PROLOGUE	 12
CHAPTER 1: Beginning	 13
CHAPTER 2: Handsworth	 27
CHAPTER 3: Ever Changing World	 50
CHAPTER 4: School Life	 65
CHAPTER 5: Responsibility	 84
CHAPTER 6: Wednesfield	 101
CHAPTER 7: Dramatic Changes	 126
CHAPTER 8: Birth	 137
CHAPTER 9: Contrast	 144
CHAPTER 10: Church	 148
CHAPTER 11: Curve Ball	 157
CHAPTER 12: Disappearance	 167
CHAPTER 13: Lost	 182
CHAPTER 14: Betrayal	 194
EPILOGUE	 202

Forgiveness: The Journey to Healing the Heart

PROLOGUE

This is a true account of my life journey. I have aimed to recount every experience that I have been through as accurately as possible. Some events many seem wholly impossible. I have always had the ability to remember certain early events. My memories of my early years are so accurate that I have even been able to tell my mum what she was wearing and the colour of the dress or whatever item she had on at the time. My mum's reply is usually 'how do you remember that? You would have only been about 18 months old at the time.' For me this was normal. My family accepted that that was just the way that I am. There are still many family and friends that can testify to these things and many more of my life journey.

Audreia Josephs

CHAPTER 1
BEGINNINGS

Though I was born in the United Kingdom, my story begins in Jamaica. I am first generation, born in the UK to Jamaican parents. Both of my parents are originally from the parish of Portland, Jamaica.

My father's brother John came to the UK first and then sent for his younger brother, my father Martan, in 1958. Mother had already had two children with my father in Jamaica, but my parents had a volatile relationship. My father had been a local policeman in Jamaica. He stood taller than six feet, with dark mocha bronze skin, hazelnut eyes, and hair like silk. My mum meanwhile was a petite woman, part Indian, part maroon dark chocolate beauty with long flowing hair. She had been only 14 years old when she met my father.

My mum's mother Doris Miller had died when my mum was only six years old. Her maternal grandparents Margret and John Miller had raised her, but her life was not a happy one. She suffered many traumas and dramas as she grew up.

It was said that when my father had first set eyes on my mum, he found himself in the area every day seeking her out. My father took

Forgiveness: The Journey to Healing the Heart

a liking to my mum and moved her in to his mother Urcella's house. Not long after, she gave birth to my sister Gen, followed shortly by the birth of my brother Jim.

Father was a player and a womaniser, facts which did not escape my mother. Women used to walk past her home, taunting her by saying that they were his latest lovers. My grandmother would not put up with that kind of behaviour and ran out and chased these women away. Apparently my mum was having weekly fights with either my father or one of his other women. One day my mum had had enough of my father's womanising ways, so they split up.

Both my parents moved on with their own lives separately. My mum went on to have twins with someone else, a girl and boy called Jane and Robert, and then she had another daughter called June with another man. My father went to the UK.

Father had a woman in Jamaica that he was very fond of and had planned to bring her to England. He had processed her paperwork, and her ticket had been booked, but word had got to him that this woman had found another man and was pregnant by him. He was angry, and he was even angrier that he would lose a substantial amount of money. My father's older brother John was very fond of my mum and his niece and nephew in Jamaica, so he suggested that my father help my mum get to England instead. My father agreed and proceeded to get her paperwork processed. However, my father neglected to tell his brother that he had already met and was living part-time with someone else.

Audreia Josephs

My mother had met her father for the first time two weeks before she left Jamaica. Only because he found out that she was leaving for England did he introduce himself. He had lived in the same area as she did but had never taken the time out of his life to get to know his daughter. Her mother had died at the age of 26 when my mum was only six years old. My mum had thought that her father had died, too. My mum arrived in England on the 9th of March in 1960. Upon arriving in Heathrow Airport, there was no one to meet her. Armed only with an address and seven pounds sterling that my father had sent to her, she took a train from Heathrow to Birmingham New Street Station, where she got a taxi to Darlaston in the West Midlands and the house where my father and his brother John lived in rented rooms.

Though my mum was now with him in England, Father proceeded as he always had, living life by his own rules. Sometimes he was at home, and other times he was missing for days at a time. The fights started again. My mum is a fighter, and though she is small and petite, she could draw blood from my father. It was all too much, the nightly arguments and fights. The house was owned by an Asian family who drew the line one day when they saw my father covered in blood. Both of my parents were asked to leave. During 1960s in Britain, it was very difficult to find accommodation. There were signs in windows stating, 'No Blacks. No dogs. No Irish. No children.' In the middle of all of this turmoil, my mother found out that she was pregnant with me. My father went on the missing list, so my mother told his brother John

Forgiveness: The Journey to Healing the Heart

and his wife Miss Mary that she was pregnant. She also talked to them about my father's behaviour. My Uncle John was upset with my father. He pointed out that my mother hadn't even been given the chance to acclimate in the UK before having to contend with a baby as well. When John saw his brother again, he told my father that my mother was pregnant and that he was disgusted with my father. The brothers fell out, and my father stopped speaking to his older brother.

Mum found a job in a pickle onion factory and did not want anyone there to know that she was now an unmarried mother and pregnant. She had had a fellow Jamaican friend who was also pregnant and without a husband, and this friend had told the people that she worked for that she was having a baby. When her son was born, government services came to the hospital and took the baby away, putting him up for adoption. My mum said that they had both cried for days. There was a big stigma in 1960s England about unmarried mothers. If the government found out about a pregnancy, they would take away the baby and put him up for adoption. So the black community would try to keep these things under wraps. My mum proceeded to hide her pregnancy by banning her belly down - tying a length of cloth around her belly so that it looked flat - and wearing oversized clothes.

One day my mum went to work as usual, but when she got back home, she entered an empty house. My father had apparently come back to their shared rented room during the day and cleared out every last piece of furniture that he had bought for her or with her. He took things that she had bought for herself with her own money as well. He even took the piss pot - they called it chemie or potty. There were hardly any indoor flushing toilets in terrace houses in 1960s. So he quite literally took everything. She was seven months pregnant at the time.

Mum had known my father could not be trusted, so a few months earlier she had contacted her brother Grantley - or Grant as everyone else called him - in Jamaica and had started the process of getting him to the UK to support her. He would be there to support her in place of my father. On Wednesday the 21st of June, 1961, at about 5:30PM, my mum was having a bath and felt a mild pain, from left to right. She stepped out of the bath, and I made my grand entrance into the world on the bathroom floor.

I have to pause here for a moment......... Born on a bathroom floor????? Had to be me. There's nothing normal about me. It's what's made me who I am.

The ambulance came and took my mum and me to the hospital. When we arrived, my mother said the nurses happily told her that I was born with a silver spoon in my mouth, meaning that I would be lucky because I was born on the longest day of the year, the summer solstice. Uncle Grant came to the hospital as my stand-in father - my mum had brought a wedding ring and pretended that her brother was her husband. A man who worked at the pickle factory with my mum

Forgiveness: The Journey to Healing the Heart

had a baby around the same time that I had been born. He came to the hospital to visit his wife and new child and was most shocked to see my mum with a baby in the bed across from his wife. 'Ruby,' (my mother's birth name is Rubena, and the people that she worked with called her Ruby) he said to my mum, 'I didn't know that you were having a baby!' No one at the factory had known, and when he went back to work and told his work colleagues, they too were all surprised and shocked. My mum had been going in to work every day without complaint or a belly, so no one had suspected a thing. It looked like mum's pregnancy disguise had worked.

I did not meet my father until I was two years old.

As I mentioned before, my mum is of mixed Indian heritage; so was my father. His mother's father was Scottish. My paternal grandmother Urcella came from an area in Portland, called Cooper's Hill. Both of my parents have what is termed as 'good hair', though it is not a term to which I subscribe. My mum did not understand why her British-born child did not have the same hair quality her parents. I had wooly hair, but she wanted me to have long flowing hair, and her dissatisfaction with my hair would remain for many years. I was almost two years old when one day she bumped into a work collogue with his daughter. His daughter had the long flowing hair that she wanted me to have, so she asked him what shampoo he used in his daughter's hair. He told her what his wife used in her hair, and where she could buy it. Mum went and bought the shampoo that very day.

Audreia Josephs

She washed my hair with the shampoo, and the very next day my hair started falling out in large bunches. This continued for a few days, until only small tuffs of hair was left on my head. I cried, she cried, and we cried. The shampoo was called Selsun. I never forgot the name of that shampoo. Even now when my mum cannot remember the name, I remind her of the name of it. My hair didn't really grow back until 40 years later.

    Not long after that I caught whooping cough, or the 100-day cough. At the time, there was a mass whooping cough epidemic in the UK. Lots of children were dying, and many were the same age as I was. When I had a coughing attack, I would not be able to breathe for what seemed like hours. I would use all my energy to try to breathe before I would pass out. I thought I was going to die. My mum did her best to help me breathe, using old remedies from Jamaica, like putting me in front of a bowl of hot water and covering my head over it with a towel. Mum also made herbal drinks for me. Miraculously I started getting better and stronger day by day, and before long I was back to my old, playful self.

    My early childhood life with my mum was wonderful. I was a very inquisitive child, and I had great comprehension. All the people that met me marvelled at how intelligent for my age they thought I was. Many even predicted that I would go to university. Little did I know that life circumstances would prevent that prediction from coming true for nearly 30 years. Throughout that period of my childhood, I

Forgiveness: The Journey to Healing the Heart

never felt that I missed out on anything. Mum had a personal dress maker called Vergie with whom she had all of her dresses made. What I loved the most was that after Vergie had made my mum's dress, she would make me a dress out of the leftover fabric. Mum loved the community interaction of house parties. She would take me along, and if anyone objected to my presence at the party, mum would say that if I was not welcomed then neither was she. With both of us in our matching dresses, I somehow became the star of these parties. I soon found my first talent: I could dance. I did all the latest dance moves, and I was very good at doing a 1960s dance called the twist. It seemed that I could do it well, as people were even willing to pay me. They even requested my dancing. I loved dancing to 'My Boy Lollipop' by Millie Small; it was my favourite dancing song. Little did I know that that was the start of my entrepreneurial journey. My mum saved all of the money that I was given, and years later it would enable her to pay the deposit on our first family home. I was young, and we were happy.

One day in a conversation with a lady called Little, my mum found out where my father was living. Even though my father was living in the same town as we were, she had not seen him since she was seven months pregnant and he had moved all of the furniture out. It was now 1963, and I was two years old. And suddenly, there was something different about my mum. It didn't feel normal. She would get me dressed. I was always well dressed - my mother would have it no other way. Matching red dress, coat and bonnet with navy blue

Audreia Josephs

velvet trim. But her face looked mad as hell while getting me ready for this mystery trip. She did not tell me where we were going. I heard her saying words about yuh fardah. I had heard those words before, but I didn't understand them. Mum was walking fast now, and my little two-year-old legs were trying to keep up with her. I might have only been two years old, but I could tell that this was no ordinary day. We always used to talk during our walks together, but today was different. She spoke under her breath, with no smiles, and sometimes even pulled me along by my arm.

    She rang the bell to a large house that I had never seen before. Oh, yes, she was mad. Someone opened the door, and she went in and started shouting 'Nadab' 'Nadab' - my father's nickname. Not knowing which room was his, she just kept shouting at the top of her voice. He heard her commotion and came out of one of the rooms. He said, 'Enid, (a name that only family and close friends called her) stop mek up noise.' Stop making noise. This got her even madder. 'Stop mek up noise.' 'See yuh daughter here? Yes me had ah daughter for you. You did not even came back to find out what kind of baby I had.' She launched into a tirade of verbal abuse. I was standing there in my finest looking at this man that I clearly did not know, my mum screaming at the top of her voice. I had never seen her like that. My little heart was beating so fast, I could hardly breathe. Had I got the whooping back? I couldn't breathe. I started breathing erratically. They stopped arguing to attend to me. The man that had been arguing

Forgiveness: The Journey to Healing the Heart

with my mum went and got me a glass of water, and I was given a chair. This time he looked at me intensely. Mum started off again. 'Ah yuh cause dis.' I was slowly calming down when we all heard the cry of a baby come from the room from which my father had come. My mum looked incensed. 'Yuh have nother baby???? You have never come and find out what baby I had, you have never given me a penny for this child and gone have next pickney. You should be ashamed of yourself. What about the other children in Jamaica?' My father replied, 'Every week I have to send money home for them. They live with my mother, and I send money and barrel of goods home for them.' Mum continued, 'What about your daughter here living in England?' He took another look at me and said, 'I have a son, your brother.'

    With that we left. In one day, I had both met the man who was my father and found out that I had a brother. My mum was never the same with me after that visit. Our relationship had changed drastically.

    Mum got on with her life, and she met a man who seemed to bring a smile to her face. He was a well-dressed and handsome man named Mr. Slick. At my age, I didn't understand what beautiful and handsome meant, but I knew what I saw when other people saw the two of them together. He was very friendly, playful and kind to me. He used to stay over with my mum from time to time, and then one day he started living with us. After we had gone to my father's house, my mother became less and less gentle toward me, but this new man was fun. We played games and laughed most of the time.

Audreia Josephs

One day my mum was downstairs in the kitchen, and Mr. Slick and I were playing and eating cream crackers under the sheets. We were still living in rented rooms. He pointed to his manhood and told me that I should touch it. I was only three years old at the time, and I had never seen anything like that before. He said, 'Shhhh, touch it.' I put my little finger out to touch it and then pulled back. He said not to tell anyone, it was our game. Then we continued laughing. I had no idea that what had happened was called grooming, and I never told anyone about it.

Mum gave birth in June 1965 to my brother Miles. I was ten days away from my fourth birthday and was so excited to have a little brother. He was so cute, with his masses of shiny, jet-black curls. I, on the other hand, still only had very short hair.

I looked more like a boy than my brother did. One morning I woke up early to look at my lovely baby brother, but what greeted me was frightening. I looked in my brother Miles' cot. It was covered in blood. I screamed. My mum woke up. She looked in the cot and screamed as well. While we were sleeping, a rat had gotten into Miles' cot and eaten through pieces of his flesh. Miles had slept through all of it. My mum rushed Miles to the hospital, where they cleaned and dressed Miles' wounds. He was okay in the end.

When I was four years old, my father had still not come to visit me, so yet again my mum found out where he would be - this time, at which pub he would be drinking. She promptly marched me up there,

Forgiveness: The Journey to Healing the Heart

pushed me in front of him and shouted so everyone could hear. 'You have never come and visited your daughter. You have never given me a pound for her. I am doing this all by myself.' Everyone tried to calm her down. I stood in the middle of the pub, wide-eyed and terrified. Someone gave me a packet of pork scratchings to eat. I think my mum's cussin and telling off in the pub worked because the next day my father came to visit me. He came armed with a gift. When he produced this gift, I screamed and ran. It was a doll. No ordinary doll; it was a black doll. It was 1965, and I had only ever played with white dolls. I had never seen a black doll before. The sight of my father trying to hand me that doll sent me running and screaming. I hid behind my mum. 'Yuh nuh see say she frighten?' my mother told my father. 'Can't you see that she's frightened?' The doll was about three feet tall. She wore a red checkered dress, with a blue and white checkered apron, white ankle socks, and shiny, black buckled shoes. The doll had black curly hair just like my new baby brother, a skin colour that was closer to black, and a face that now that I think about it looked more like the bride of Chucky. If you have ever seen that film, you will know what I mean. There is no way a black person made that doll. Now that I look back, I am truly grateful that my father went out of his way to bring his black daughter a black doll. But at the time, I did not appreciate it at all.

What came after the black doll event was far more traumatic than anything I had experienced before in my young life. I heard

Audreia Josephs

both of my parents speaking. My father was saying, 'If you cut it off, it will grow back.' 'Don't be so stupid,' mum said. My father was very insistent that his plan would work. 'No,' my mum said. I had no idea that they were talking about me. When my mum went to work, she would leave me and my baby brother with a child minder; and so one day my father found out who my child minder was and where she lived and came round. I was so excited to see him. 'Do you know who I am? I am yuh fardah,' he said to me. That would always be his opening line to me. He took me to the corner shop and bought me some sweets. I felt so grown up holding my daddy's hand. Because he was so tall, people kept staring at us. I felt so proud. For the first time in my young life, I felt like I was truly his daughter. As soon as we got back to the child minder's home, he got a chair for me to sit in. He put a towel around my shoulders and took a shiny item from a bag. I had never anything like it and wondered what it was used for. I was about to find out. He started cutting what little hair I had left on my head. I screamed and cried for him to stop. 'Sit still,' he kept saying in his rough voice. I cried every time I saw the bits of my hair on the floor. I cried all day until my mum got back from work. When she saw my head she went ballistic. 'I gwine kill dat fucker.' The amount of swear words I learnt that day, just by listening to my mother's rant. Even the child minder got cussed out. I don't know if she ever found my father that day, but he was still alive later, so I guess not. My father had broken the short-lived bond that we had made earlier in that day

Forgiveness: The Journey to Healing the Heart

walking to the shop. I was left heart broken, sad and confused by my father again. After that, it would be another nine years before I would see my father again.

Audreia Josephs

CHAPTER 2
Handsworth

Mum gave birth to another one of Mr. Slick's children, my sister Mary. I was five and half years old and had not long been in school. Living in a small rented room would no longer be an option with a family of three children and two adults. Mum's brother uncle Grant had moved to Birmingham, and he wanted his sister closer to him, so the adults decided we would move to be closer together. One day I got home from school to see that everything had been wrapped and packed up. No one had said anything to me. A big van came and put all of our lives in its boot. I was told to get in the back of the van with my mum, brother and baby sister. As soon as we stepped in, the doors were shut. No windows. I couldn't see out, so I had no way of knowing where we were going. I tried to ask my mum where we were going, but she just said sit down and be quiet. Her tone was becoming sharper with me daily. 'Yuh ah big gal, sid down, yuh chat too much.' (You're a big girl, sit down, you talk too much.) This was not the first or last time that I would hear that statement - my inquisitiveness wasn't appreciated any longer. The days of our matching dresses were long gone.

Forgiveness: The Journey to Healing the Heart

After what seemed like hours in the back of that van, it finally stopped moving. I couldn't wait for those big doors to open. The doors opened and there was Mr. Slick and my mum's brother Uncle Grant, my stand-in father. Uncle Grant lived with a lady nicknamed Sweetie. Sweetie had children from a previous marriage and two children with my Uncle Grant. They lived in a big house in Grove Lane in Handsworth. They rented out rooms, and we now had one of them. No matter what anyone has to say about Handsworth now, you should have seen it when I was a child growing up there. It was beautiful. So now we were going to live with my uncle and aunt.

Mum didn't have a lot of patience with me, and I was always getting slapped for something. I was always asking questions, climbing on something, or just being a mischievous six-year-old child. At times I would wish that I was more like my younger brother and sister. They were so quiet, to the point of being almost being invisible.

Auntie Sweetie had a deep love for me and would ask my mother why she always slapped me. My mother's reply was 'She too rude.' Auntie Sweetie and Uncle Grant got married, and I had the chance to be a flower girl at their wedding. I was measured for my flower girl dress. The dresses were all made within a few days, and then it was time for the wedding. I had a headband, a beautiful dress and a basket with flowers to carry. I did my part. I walked down the aisle with the other flower girls and smiled. My mother was a bridesmaid. Throughout the wedding, every time I looked at my mother she would glare at me. I didn't care. I felt beautiful, like a princess in the stories they told us at school. After the wedding, the reception took place in my future school, Grove Lane Juniors and Infants. I ran around the playground with the other children. We ate cake, fruit, sandwiches, sweets; I even received a bit of wine from my Uncle Grant. I was so busy having fun that I didn't see my mum come up behind me, grab my arm and pull me to the side to pinch me really hard. I was so shocked that I didn't even cry at first. 'Go sid down, yuh run up and down too much, and ah get ina people way.' My Auntie Sweetie's sister Cassie saw what happened and walked toward us. 'It's alright, Enid,' she said to my mother. 'I will keep an eye on her for you.' As soon as my mother turned her back, Cassie gave me a big embrace. As soon as she hugged me, I felt like I had been hugged by angel with wings. Though I had met her on a few occasions previously, this was the start of a special friendship between Auntie Cassie and me.

    Mum had taken to calling us by nicknames. As a very small girl, my name was Tunde. I have no idea where she got that name from, and no one else in the family ever called me by that name. When I got older, I looked up the meaning of the name that my mother had called me. This is what I found out about the name: Tunde is a unisex name, originally a Yoruba name for a native of Nigeria, which also means 'return'.

    Living in Grove Lane was so much fun. I loved living in Grove Lane because it was so close to the park. When we first came to

Forgiveness: The Journey to Healing the Heart

Birmingham, there was a fair in Handsworth Park. There, I saw marching bands, girls and boys brigade, girl guides and boys scouts. I was amazed to see all of these people marching through the park. They marched through the park and on to the main road. I loved all the uniforms. It was the first time that I had ever had candy floss. The lake in the park had small boats on it. There was a brass band playing, on the bandstand in the middle of the park. There were fun fair rides, and it was all so exciting to see. Despite the growing dislike from my mother and the threatening presence of Mr. Slick, I had cousins and the other boarders' children as playmates and friends everywhere I seemed to turn. It was in this house that I had made a friend, a girl called Janet, who was one year younger than I was. She became my lifelong friend, and we were dear friends for over 40 years until she passed away in 2013. I was sent to Grove Lane Junior and Infants School. I was a friendly girl, and I got on very well with my peers. Many of the friends I made in that school continue to be friends today. One of the first friends I made was called Yvonne Henry. We shared the same last name, and so we started telling everyone that we were sisters. Yvonne lived on Mostyn Road, which was just across the road from our school. I used to walk Yvonne home, and we both always got into mischief together. Yvonne had a younger sister called Marilyn and an older sister called Audrey Henry, the same name as mine. Later in our lives, our names would be the cause for a very funny confusion.

    I became aware that though my mum was rough with me, there

were other gentle women who loved me just because they did. One such woman was Ivy Drysdale. My mum had to work and could not carry me to school, and thought that me crossing roads at six years old was too dangerous. I had gone to school by myself at first, but I had fallen off the back of an open door bus and damaged my face (In 1960s, the buses did not have doors at the back. A driver in front drove the bus while a conductor collected the money. If you missed the bus, you could run up and jump on at the back.) So my mother asked a neighbour's son to take me to school. He was older than I was but his senior school was close to my own. Mrs. Drysdale had three sons and no daughters, so I became an adopted daughter, and her son Donavan became my big brother. Years later I choose Mrs. Drysdale to become my first born child's godmother. The Drysdales had their own house, which was not shared. When I finished school, she would let me stay at her house until my mother got back from work. She would feed me all kinds of goodies, plus she was a very good cook. She was such a kind woman to me.

    In 1967 I was six years old. One day my mum's most precious treasured gold watch went missing. This was a watch that she had saved up to buy when she first came to England. It was 18-carat gold. She looked everywhere and could not find it. She asked Mr. Slick if he had seen it. His reply was no, he hadn't. I used to play in her jewellery box, so she asked me if I had taken it out of the box. I replied that no I hadn't, but somehow she came to the conclusion that I must have

Forgiveness: The Journey to Healing the Heart

taken it to school. My mum told me of her plan. She was going to beat me until I admitted that I had stolen it. So she beat me every day after school for two solid weeks. My mother beat me until I wet myself and lost my voice. I confessed to stealing the watch, knowing that I had not stolen it but hoping that the beatings would end. I was in terror of going home because I knew that I was going home for my daily beating. I was in so much fear that I started sucking my thumb. I had never sucked my thumb as a baby, and now here I was searching for the only comfort that I could find. I had marks all over my skin from those beatings. She even contacted the school, to find out if they had seen me with the watch. Up to now, she had only ever slapped or pinched me. This was something different.

About a month after my two weeks of beatings had ended; my mother was searching through Mr. Slick's pocket and found the missing watch. I grew up watching my mother search through the pockets of any man that she was with at the time. I think that she was looking for evidence of infidelity. She never fully trusted of any man. How could she after my father? She told me that she was sorry for beating me. I told her that I had been telling the truth. This was not the last time my mother would take the word of a man over my word. She argued with Mr. Slick about finding the watch in his pocket, but all he had wanted to know was why she had searched his pockets.

We lived a few doors away from the swimming baths, which was on the corner of Hinstock Road and Grove Lane. I loved those

Audreia Josephs

swimming baths because I learnt to swim there. Until this point in my life, I hadn't thought that I was good at anything except dancing. For me the world worked in a different way. Even at school I had major problems because I was left-handed. When I used my left hand to write, the teacher would come over to me and put my pencil into my right hand. Every time I tried to eat my school dinner, the dinner ladies would come and switch the way I held my knife and fork around the other way. But swimming was my joy. It made no difference if I was left -or right-handed. In swimming, I found something that put all of us children in a level space, and I excelled in it. The first time I got in the water I loved it, and I promptly made up my mind that I was going to swim. Most black mothers didn't want their daughters to go swimming because of the chlorine. It is not kind on black hair. Chlorine causes the hair to fall off. Many of the girls that I knew did not attend swimming for that very reason. I, on the other hand, didn't have much hair to worry about. Finally there was a benefit to not having much hair. I was so good that I went on to win medals and a few awards for my swimming. I also got a free swimming pass. From the age of seven all the way to fifteen, I never paid to swim because I always won my free swimming pass. I am proud to say that I learnt to swim in the swimming bath where most of the schools in the area brought their students to learn to swim. What the teachers didn't know was that if any of us needed to urinate, we would all just urinate in the swimming pool. I also did my share of urinating in the

Forgiveness: The Journey to Healing the Heart

swimming pool. So I learnt to swim at the age of seven in a pool of piss. To this day, I love swimming, but I am not a lover of public swimming baths. And my distaste for them becomes even worse if I know that school children swim there. My parents could not swim, though they came from Jamaica. In fact most of the people that I have met from the Caribbean cannot swim. No other member of my family took to swimming nor had the same passion that I had for water.

    I was never sure what happened to the house in Grove Lane. I came home from school one day, and the whole house had been emptied into moving vans and boxes. Everyone was moving out. No one told us kids anything. The grown-ups spoke to each other, but even with my eavesdropping, I couldn't pick up any information as to why we were all moving out. What I did find out was that we were not moving very far. The van took our furniture, and we walked to our new house, a very large house that my Uncle Grant and Auntie Sweetie had just brought. We were going to be living there as well. Whitehall Road was now my new home. But Whitehall Road would bring its own set of problems for me. Grove Lane Junior and Infants was a bit further away, and so now they were talking about changing my school. I had just gotten settled into my school. I had been there for about 12 months, and I had made friends. Changing schools and moving house also meant that I was not going to see my adopted brother Donavan or his mother Mrs. Drysdale. In the rush of moving, I had not been given the chance to say goodbye to them. Meanwhile, my best friend Janet and her family had also moved to somewhere else, but I had no idea where. Little did I know that a few years later we would meet again.

Some of my cousins had been going to a school called Farm Street Junior and Infants. So it was agreed by the grown-ups that I, too, would attend that school. I was so upset that I cried, but no one cared enough to listen to my pleas. **That day I learnt that no matter how much you cry or display your grief, you have to suck it up and act like a big girl.** I started my new school and tried to adjust. It was okay. Some of my male cousins attended the same school, it was at least bearable.

My new school was in Hockley, not far from the Hockley flyover. Under the flyover was a large circular concourse with various subway exits. You could walk from one side of Hockley to the other using these exits. After school this concourse area became our adventure playground. We would challenge each other to see who could run highest up the wall. At its highest point, this wall was about 12 feet high. I loved running around the whole perimeter. I could even be found to be balancing on the safety rails. The bus station was on the other side of the road.

I was not the best student. I found it hard to grasp the schools teaching style and always fell behind all the other children. Writing was my key problem. I am left-handed. No matter what I was doing, the teachers always tried to get me to use my right hand. I would become so frustrated with it all that I would stop trying. I would put

Forgiveness: The Journey to Healing the Heart

my pencil down and refuse to do any work. They thought that I was being stubborn and called my mum in to state this point. Mum did not like being called into school because of me. She had to take time out of her job because of me. I knew what was coming when I got home. Don't they understand I cannot write with my right hand because I am left-handed? **I never understood that anger left unattended in a seven-year-old child would be a dangerous thing to grow up with.** When I got home from school, my mum had not returned from work. She had to work overtime to make up for the time she had had to take off to come to my school. I went in to the garden to play. I was in a world of my own when I heard 'Yuh out ya ah play ina yuh school uniform!!!!!!!' I stood rooted to the spot. Not only had I caused her to come to my school, take time out of work, work overtime, but now here I was playing in my school uniform. She dragged me upstairs to our room, promptly grabbed Mr. Slick's belt and proceeded to beat me back into her reality. She kept saying, 'I send you to school to learn and you don't want to learn. I will teach you with this belt. Plus you have mess up your school uniform.' WACK WACK WACK. The belt sounded on my tender seven-year-old skin.

I still refused to write in class. My reading was not much better. If I tried anything and I did not get the instant results that I wanted, I would stop trying. **During this time, I learnt my giving up skills.** It was not the last time that I would be beaten for playing in my school uniform either.

Audreia Josephs

They all had no idea that I was learning. But what was I learning? So far I had learned anger and how to give up. And that you could be beaten mercilessly if you did not follow the rules. Or if someone did not believe you. I learnt that I was on my own. No one was going to save me. My father never came to visit me. I lost trust in my mother. Both anger and the skill of giving up grew up with me and pretended to be my best and only true friends. Those skills later on in my life would serve me unfaithfully.

Despite all this, I loved being an older sister. I loved my little brother Miles and my baby sister Mary. They were the ideal brother and sister. I was expected to help out with them, a job with which I had no problem. My brother Miles developed a skin rash on his feet, and they had to be washed at regular intervals and rubbed in ointment. This job needed to be done at least seven times a day, and it became my job to do it. I didn't mind at all, and I would make up songs and sing to him, or just make him laugh, while I worked. We called him 'tender foot'. Despite his condition, he was incredibly strong. No one had ever seen a child as strong as my brother Miles. He could lift more than his own body weight and would often demonstrate his super-human strength, saying 'Mummy, I'm going to lift you up!' And he would actually life her up off the ground while she would just keep saying, 'Miles, put me down.' He thought it was funny. He was only four years old at the time. My sister Mary was a very cute but ghostly-quiet child. All she would do was smile and stare. She spoke in a kind of whisper,

Forgiveness: The Journey to Healing the Heart

and if she got upset, she would projectile vomit. She suffered from constant nose bleeds and had to be brought to the hospital because of it. She also had a hernia, which caused her navel to protrude. Mum would use a thick rubber belt - with an old penny on her navel - to stop it from sticking out. Miles and Mary were Mr. Slick's children. They were 18 months apart in age and seemed to commutate in some kind of telepathy, something that I did not share with them. As we grew up, I always felt left out of their silent code.

One day the house next door to my Uncle Grant went up for sale. My mum decided that it would be good idea if she and Mr. Slick bought it. With the deposit paid - courtesy of me and my dancing days - and a mortgage, we had our own seven bedroom house. It was one of the largest houses on the road and right next door to our family. The two houses were mirror images of each other; they were even painted the same colour. When we had originally moved to Whitehall Road, there had been quite a few white families living there. But as the time passed, fewer and fewer white families lived there. With the white families leaving, we were able to buy the house next door. It had been previously owned by a Polish family. The house was a pre-war, five to seven bedroomed house with two bathrooms. On entering, you were met by a very small entry space, which housed the gas and electric meter. One door was in front of you, and one main door was to your right, allowing the house to be split into two flats. I was originally excited because I had thought that we would get our own rooms.

Audreia Josephs

However when we moved in, we only occupied the ground floor half of the house. Mr. Slick and my mother had rented the upstairs flat to another family. The ground floor consisted of a large hallway. On the right side of the hallway was what we called a box room pantry. I was very often locked in this very small, dark space for hours for supposed bad behaviour. A large room on the left of the hallway became the untouchable room. In black families this was the front room, the inner sanctum. A child could be killed for entering this room without permission, but more on this room later. Further ahead in the left corner was the room that was to be Mum's and Mr. Slick's. Miles, Mary and I were given a 3 by 7 foot store room with no windows for our shared bedroom. There was a bathroom, and there was a fireplace in the dining area combined with sitting room. Just off this room and to the right was the kitchen. Outside there was a coal house and an outside toilet. Our only means of keeping our homes warm in the 1960s was to use coal and a fire place. The coal man would deliver sacks of coal into the coal house. We also used our fire place to have our baths. We had a tin bathtub that my mother would place in front of a roaring fire. We would fill it up with hot water and bathe in it. Sometimes I loved making toast in front of our coal fire. We also used an oil burning heating lamp called a 'paraffin heater' to keep the bedrooms warm. We did not have wall-to-wall carpeting. Instead we had wooden floors with large gaps in it that would let the icy cold air straight into the flat. It was my job to stain, varnish and polish this wooden floor at

Forgiveness: The Journey to Healing the Heart

the weekends. The floor was covered with a rug. We did not have central or under-floor heating. Most people used coal fires, which was why 1960s Britain was dark, grey and foggy. The smoke would escape through the chimneys on top of the roof of our houses, causing smog and, eventually, fog. England was so cold at night that my siblings and I would sleep hugging each other for warmth. At times it was so cold that we would have ice on the inside of our windows, and we would draw shapes in the ice on the windows. The milkman would deliver the milk to our doorstep, but by the time we got to it, it would be frozen solid. It was so cold then that we got more than four feet of severe snow fall. There were times that we would open our front door and be unable to leave because of the snow. The snow was so deep that it came up to our knees, and on a few occasions I lost my Wellington boots in the snow. My foot would go down and come up without the boot. It was so cold that at times I would rush in to the house to get warm, by putting my hands and feet in front of the coal fire. I would end up with chilblains. It would itch and itch so much that I would scratch and scratch at it until it started to bleed. A chilblain itch is severe, and afterward I would always wish that I had allowed my blood to circulate before I threw my hands and feet in front of the fire.

    As I mentioned before, the front room was my mum's personal little world, her front room. It consisted of a glass cabinet set in the corner, which contained all of the best wine glasses and the bone china tea set. There was also a German music centre, called a 'Bluespot',

Audreia Josephs

which we affectionately called the Gram. There was three piece sofa, and ornaments all around the room, most of which I had brought back from school trips. A centre table held more ornaments, a rubber plant, and some artificial flowerers in a vase. A drinks trolley housed white rum and various other strong drinks. A picture of Jamaica decorated the wall, as did a picture of a white Jesus and some bible verses. My mother kept this room locked with a key; it was mainly used when grown-ups came to the house or whenever there was a party. No child could ever go in to that room without an adult. If attempted, the said child could face uncertain death.

My mum used to go in on a Sunday and listen to Jim Reeves, a popular singer in the Caribbean community. She would play his album over and over again, while she cooked our Sunday dinner of boiled chicken, rice and peas. You could always tell what day it was based on what we were having for dinner. Monday was leftovers from Sunday's dinner. Tuesday was corn beef and rice. Wednesday was tins of Campbell's soup. Thursday was pilchards and fried dumpling. Friday was fish and chips. Saturday was mutton or beef soup. And we would always eat on white enamel plates with a blue rim and drank from our enamel mugs. Meanwhile Whitehall Road was always party central. Almost every week, my uncle and auntie had a party next door. But the requests for me to dance had long since ended as I got older.

In 1970 our mother took us to see a matinee for the first time in our lives. I was so excited. Previously, we had only walked past

Forgiveness: The Journey to Healing the Heart

the cinema; we had never gone in. I was so curious to see what the inside of the building looked like. So we got dressed up in our best clothes and headed to the Elite Cinema on Soho Road, where they were showing a Beatles animated film called The Yellow Submarine. There were a lot of families seated in there, all ready to enjoy the film. Mum bought us popcorn, ice cream and drinks. Miles, Mary and I really enjoyed our first cinema experience.

When my brother Miles started at Farm Street School with me, it was my job to bring him to school. I also continued to care for his tender feet. I didn't mind coming out of my own class several times a day to attend to my little brother. In fact it made me feel grown up and responsible, and since I still refused to learn to write, it was a good escape. The teachers admired how well I cared for my brother though I was very young myself. I knew the drill.

One day the school choir sang in assembly, and I loved hearing the sound. I quickly sought to find out how I could become a part of it, and it was not long before I joined the choir. I learned that they were famous and had been recorded for the BBC radio. I considered myself lucky to be a part of it. In singing I found a talent and passion for something that I had no idea that I could do. The best part of it was that in the choir it made no difference that I was left-handed. Meanwhile, we had started having proper Art classes in school, and no one tried to change the hand that I used for Art. Thus, I found yet another talent. I thought that I was good at Art, and best of all,the

Audreia Josephs

teacher did, too.

Though I was still a long way behind the other children in writing, reading and spelling, I was able to count. Mr. Slick had been teaching my brother Miles and me how to count. I mainly learnt how to count from watching our favourite Saturday afternoon program 'Wrestling'. I was TV obsessed as a child. On Saturdays we all sat together as a family, with biscuits, and orange squash, ready for our weekly fix. We all loved a wrestler called 'Big Daddy'. He used to knock the opponents out with his large belly. Another one of our favourite wrestlers was called 'Giant Haystack'. We didn't care about the others. Mum would shout at the TV. 'Lick him down! Hold him down!' We would all laugh. Whenever someone was on the ground, the referee would count, 'One ah, two ah, three ah, four ah, five ah, out!' While the referee counted, I would join in, 'One ah, two ah, three ah.' It was always a fun Saturday in our house, talking loud and laughing. The only problem with learning to count from the wrestling was that when I went into school one Monday morning, the teacher asked me to count in front of the other children, and I proudly stood up and counted, 'One ah, two ah, three ah, four ah.' And the other children laughed. I could not understand why they were laughing. I had counted, hadn't I? My teacher corrected me, saying, 'No, Audrey, that's not how you do it.' She counted out loud and told me to repeat it. I said that, yes, that was what I had done and began my counting again to show her that I could count. 'One ah, two ah, three ah.' My class broke out in fits of laughter again. Why were they laughing at me? I was told to sit down. The teacher asked another child to stand up and count. 'One, two, three, four, five, six, seven, eight, nine, ten.' I was confused. No one was laughing at this boy, but I had done the same thing. Why had they laughed at me? Yet another lesson I was to learn and carry in life: even when you think you're right, people will laugh at you. It took me months to understand what I had been doing wrong. Mr. Slick was the one who pointed out that I had said 'ah' after each number. So I started saying the numbers out loud and kept the 'ah' silent in my head.

Growing up with Mr. Slick was fun - or so I thought. My mum used to buy a big box of biscuits for us all on Fridays. At times Mr. Slick would get Miles, Mary and me to climb all over him. The command was, 'Feed me.' We would all laugh and feed him biscuits. The biscuits were called 'shapes' because they came in all kinds of shapes, such as stars, rounds and squares. The next thing he would say to us was, 'Byah me,' meaning rock me to sleep. We did these things all the time and never saw any harm in them. Mr. Slick worked shifts, meaning that he would work from 2 o'clock in the afternoon until 10 in the evening one week and from 10 in the evening until 6 in the morning the following week. We all had to be quiet during the day while he was on the night shift so that he could sleep. Meanwhile, over our seven weeks of school holiday, I was given the job of taking care of my younger brother and sister. One day, Mr. Slick was sleeping in his room while we played as

Audreia Josephs

quietly as we could. Suddenly Mr. Slick shouted, 'Audrey, come here.' Were we too noisy? Was I going to get told off? Had I laughed too loudly? It was a hot July day. I knocked on the door because my mother had taught me to never enter a room without knocking first. Mr. Slick said, 'Come in. Where are your brother and sister?' 'Outside playing,' I said. 'Come here,' he said. I went to him. 'Lay down on the bed,' he said. I went and lay on the bed. 'I'm going to do to you what I do to your mother.'

When he had finished doing what he wanted to do to me, he gave me a small towelling cloth and told me to wipe myself. When I wiped myself, I saw blood, and said to him, 'I'm bleeding, just like mum.' My eight-year-old mind couldn't have possibly understood the difference between menstrual cycle bleeding and the end of my virginity. 'Don't tell anybody. It our secret,' he said. Mr. Slick stole my innocence that day, and a part of my mind closed down. This was not a once-off incident. I remember him calling me one day while I was in the garden playing, and I pretended not to hear him. I did not even remember this crime had been committed against me until ten years later when I gave birth to my first born son. And even when this memory tried to break through in my mind, I denied it as a figment of my imagination. Not Mr. Slick, the man I called Daddy for close to six years. I couldn't have been remembering correctly.

There was a van that used to pick up the children around the area on Sunday. The van would take us all to an old school which was

Forgiveness: The Journey to Healing the Heart

used for Sunday school. I loved the singing, the biscuits and the drinks, but when the people got in the spirit, they would knock their chairs over me. Biscuits and drinks were not enough to make me want to stay. Additionally, my little sister was scared. When I told my mum that I didn't want to go back because of the flying chairs, she told me simply that I would be going back. When I told her that Mary had cried to the point of vomiting, she let Mary stop going but continued to send Miles and me.

My little sister Mary soon started attending the same school my brother Miles and I did, so I was now also responsible for her as well. I would teach them songs, and we performed them while standing on chairs. We each had our parts in the song. We sang, 'If I had a hammer.' We sang these songs as a form of entertainment for mum and Mr. Slick, and I loved those moments.

Things continued to become uneasy in our home. Mum was always angry, and she always took it out on me. Mum and Mr. Slick began to have major problems. There were two night clubs up the road, and one called The Monty Carlo was attended by all kinds of celebrities. The other was called the Realto - later called Tasha's - and was well known for having singers and bands from Jamaica. Mr. Slick and my mother, my Uncle Grant and Auntie Sweetie and a few others used to all get dressed to the nines to spend Saturday night in the club. But now Mr. Slick started going out without my mother. When they had first met, Mr. Slick had told my mother that he was older than he

Audreia Josephs

really was, while my mother had neglected to mention her five other children back in Jamaica. So now, somehow, they had learned each other's secrets. The air was thick with their arguments. He told her that she was an old woman, with ah whole heap of kids. He screamed about how uneducated she was, that she was unable to eat with a knife and fork, that all she could do was eat with a spoon. My mother took great offence at his insults. One day my siblings and I came home from school when we heard laughing in Mum's and Mr. Slick's room. I thought, 'This is early for mum to be home!' But I got so excited that I broke our house rule of always knocking first. I opened the door, ran in, and started to shout, 'Mum........,' only to be confronted with the sight of the upstairs lodger Mrs. Mathew in bed with Mr. Slick. To this day I still see Mrs. Mathew around town. I don't think that she thinks that I still remember that day. She always smiles sweetly at me. I smile back as she asks, 'How is your mother?'

    Mr. Slick went to work on the night shift. When my mother had got home, I naively told her what I had seen that afternoon. I blurted, 'Mum, Mrs. Mathew was in your bed with daddy.' And then I saw that look that I had seen only once before when she had taken me to meet my father for the first time. She said, 'That rass. I'm gunnha poison dat fucker.' She went upstairs and cussed out Mrs. Mathew in front of her husband and children and told them all to move out of her house. I got scared. My mum used to make cornmeal porridge for our breakfast almost every morning. I was the first to get up the next morning. It

Forgiveness: The Journey to Healing the Heart

was a Saturday, so I left Miles and Mary to sleep in. My mother was in the kitchen singing - a sign that I would later recognise as dangerous. 'Good morning, Mum.' 'Morning,' she calmly replied. 'I have turned on the gezza, so the water should be hot. Go and wash and brush your teeth.' I did as instructed and went in to the bathroom to have my wash. I heard the front door open and close. Mr. Slick was home. And then, I heard voices getting louder and louder. She was cussin' at the top of her voice, and so was he. But it was what happened next that traumatised me. During the argument my mother had taken the pot of boiling hot water off of the cooker, and she threw it at Mr. Slick. I heard the loudest, ear-piercing screams from the kitchen. I ran out of the bathroom and straight to the kitchen. Miles and Mary both woke up and came running out of our room and toward the kitchen. When my siblings saw their father screaming, they both screamed and cried, too. I stood where I was in shock. Mum was saying, 'Yuh lucky mi neva put de cornmeal ina de pot yet.' Mr. Slick continued screaming while he struggled to get his white T-shirt off. I screamed. When he managed to get the shirt off, most of his skin came off with it. His body was almost pink, and part of his face was also burnt. Mr. Mathew from upstairs must have heard the screams because was soon banging on our door. Someone must have called my Uncle Grant because soon he was also banging and shouting on the door. I went and opened it for them, and Mum seemed to come back to herself, realising what she had done. I saw her face change. Our house was filled with people.

Audreia Josephs

We were pushed out of the kitchen. Mr. Slick went to the hospital and only came back a week later to pick up his clothes before he left our lives. The police never came for my mum. No one told us how the situation had been resolved or explained. I heard my mother tell someone that she could not go back to Jamaica for a holiday because if Mr. Slick's family found out that she was near they would kill her. His family had sworn vengeance on her for her actions against him. Meanwhile, with Mr. Slick gone, I had to become more responsible for my brother and sister. Soon I was doing more for them than our mother was. I gave them their baths, ironed their clothes, and made sure that they eat the food that our mother left for us.

    Mum worked every bit of overtime that she could get to keep up with the mortgage. Then one day I was playing with Miles and Mary when I heard a loud bang. Being my curious self, I rushed toward the source of the noise, where I found my mum on the ground. I thought that she was dead. She was so still. 'Mummy, Mummy!' I shouted. 'Are you alright?' She stayed still. I ran next door to get my uncle. Mum had passed out. Uncle Grant and I helped Mum into bed. Mum went to visit the doctor the very next day and was told that she was overtired and stressed. So now with my mum not able to take care of us, I was more like Miles' and Mary's mother than a big sister. They both looked to me for more and more. They became sad when they hardly saw their father. I always tried to make them smile. I told them jokes, and we used to sing songs together. I took them everywhere with me.

Forgiveness: The Journey to Healing the Heart

CHAPTER 3
Ever Changing World

I used to watch Fanny Cradock and her husband Johnny on TV. They both presented a cooking programme. I loved watching Fanny bake cakes, and I soon became interested in baking. Auntie Gertie lived next door, with my auntie and uncle. She was Auntie Sweetie's cousin. She was a very nice and kind lady. We got on very well, and I used to go next door to visit her. She would give me pop and biscuits. I used to get cooking books out of Handsworth library. I wanted to learn how to bake as soon as I could. I could not read some of the words in the cooking book, so I went over to Auntie Gertie, and she would help me read some of the words that I did not understand. I would run back over to my house to check if I had all the ingredients. I would then run back over to Auntie Gertie for any missing ingredients. I did this for years, even when I could read the cooking books myself. I would get one item from Auntie Gertie, get over to my house to my house and realise that I needed more things. Auntie Gertie used to say, 'Audrey, why can't you get everything you need from me once?' This was our running joke. I loved Auntie.

We were soon given the opportunity to attend a new Sunday

Audreia Josephs

school. It was close enough to our home that we could walk to it, and we no longer had to get the van. We started going to the Evangelical church on Waverhilll Road, just off Soho Road in front of the library. My younger siblings and I had different surnames, so I decided that when we started Sunday school there, I would tell the teachers that we had the same surname, Henry. I instructed my siblings to keep their mouth shut. I had had enough of the kids at school asking me how we were brothers and sisters but with different surnames. There was only one problem with my plan. Some of the children from our school attended the same Sunday school, which meant more questions about the surname. Meanwhile, my brother and sister sometimes forgot that they were meant to be Henry and would say the wrong name. I would glare at them. Then they would correct it. I'm sure the Sunday school teachers thought we were strange to not know our last names.

We attended a Tuesday class at the same school. Most of the helpers were white. No flying chairs here, which was a definitely improvement. Plus if you behaved and answered the questions or recited a Bible verse that you had been given to memorise, you would get tokens. These tokens could then be saved up and used at the end of the year to buy toys or sweets that the Sunday school would lay out for us. There were up to 80 children attending this Sunday school at any given time. Everyone wanted tokens, so that we could buy goodies at the end of the year. I got tokens, but not as many as some of the other children. Sometimes I kept talking or giggling with my friends when

Forgiveness: The Journey to Healing the Heart

we were meant to be quiet. I found it hard to keep still for long periods of time, and I didn't know how to keep my mouth shut. We had talent shows at our Tuesday class, and I loved the opportunity to stand in front of everyone and sing. I could play the piano a little bit and was given the opportunity to play in the talent shows. Plus you were given extra tokens, a win-win situation.

Growing up in Handsworth, I was surrounded by some of the most amazing people. On Wednesdays we would attend Bible class across the road from my house. The white lady called Doris hosted these classes. All the children attending these classes called her Auntie Doris. Auntie Doris was a Christadelphian. She had seen that the children in the area needed an outlet and kindly opened her doors to any and all of them. We had cooking classes and Bible lessons at Auntie Doris's. We also attended another cooking class, two roads around the corner from our house, on a Monday evenings. This was where I learned to make toffee and biscuits and to bake cakes. When it was bonfire night, we also made toffee apples. All of these beautiful people opened their homes to us, with no kind of government funding. These were their private homes.

More and more I was finding reasons to like school. I loved gymnastics, finding that I was also good at that. I was so very flexible that I could twist my body into the strangest positions, like putting my foot on top of my head. I soon made friends with a girl called Maureen. Up until this point, I had made friends with only a few girls, but

Audreia Josephs

Maureen and I clicked. She had just come to my school from another school. She loved everything that I loved, and I loved everything she loved. Maureen was very patient and kind. The best part of being friends with Maureen was that she lived close to my house, on Villa Road, which was only two roads away from my house. Maureen and I would always sit in the middle of the class - not at the front and not quite at the back. I had been having problems seeing the blackboard for some time. Whenever the teacher used to write on the blackboard, I would copy what Maureen had written. I found that I was unable to see the writing on the blackboard. By now the teachers had given up trying to get me to write with my right hand. Maureen didn't mind. This continued for some time, until one day I got caught copying Maureen's work and was asked to explain myself to the headmistress Miss Gower. I was sent to her office, and I tried to explain that I could not see the backboard clearly. My mother was sent a letter. I was not sure what was in the letter, but my mother made an appointment for me to go to the optician to get an eyesight test. There was one not far from Thornhill Road and not far from our house, on Soho Road. It was called Bishop's Optician. I was eight, almost nine, years old. Mr. Bishop put things on my eyes and said, 'Can you see those letters?' He continued like this for about 20 minutes, and then he said, 'Let's go outside and speak to your mother.' 'She needs glasses,' 'She is short-sighted,' he told my mother, 'They would be ready in two weeks.' The two weeks passed, and I went with my mum to get my glasses. And

Forgiveness: The Journey to Healing the Heart

then, shock of shocks, the frames were pink and as round as Harry Potter's and the lenses were incredibly thick. Apparently when I was growing up, no one cared about children's glasses design. They were the best we could get with the National Health Service; they were free. My mum was fine with them. Of course she was! She didn't have to wear them. So now here I was, plagued with another giant sign. Not only did I still have hair like a boy, but now I wore bright pink, Coke-bottled glasses. You would be considered a special needs child back in the 60s and 70s if you wore glasses. I would forever hate attending the optician because every time I received a new pair of glasses, the lenses continued to get thicker and thicker. I hated wearing the glasses because people always stared at me. I felt ugly every time I looked at myself in the mirror. The first day I wore my glasses to school, I ended up in a fight. A boy called me four-eyes, and someone else called me the Milky bar kid. There was a popular advertisement out in the 1970s for a white milk chocolate bar called Milky Bar. The boy who was in this advertisement wore a similar type of glasses as I now did. It was not the only time that I would be called four-eyes or the Milky bar kid, but for those who were brave enough to call me those names were soon sure to never say either to me again after I had exacted my anger on them. I got my mum's fighting gene.

In 1971, my whole world would change. The government introduced a whole new money system called a decimal monitory system. People had to get rid of their old money, our old pennies,

Audreia Josephs

shillings, and pounds. Now I knew that our old six pence was now worth 2½ pence. One shilling was now worth 10 pence. Everyone in the country had to get used to the new money. They tried to teach us in school, but most of the children couldn't seem to understand it. I knew that I would work it out when I needed to buy sweets. I had eaten so many sweets that I now had a few holes in my teeth, and so my mother decided to carry and Miles, Mary and me off to the dentist. This was our first ever visit to a dentist, whose office was on Soho Hill, next to the postal sorting office. I let Miles and Mary go first. They were very good; I did not hear one sound from them. Now when it came to my turn, I told them that I was not going to sit in the chair. I had looked all around the room. Too many shiny and sharp instruments. I had no idea how they would use those instruments, but I decided that they would not use them on me. Mother gave me the sideway glance. The dentist tried his very best to get me to sit in the chair. I kept refusing. Two of his assistants now tried to get me into the chair, but I kept pulling away from them. Two more people came in the room. My mouth hurt from the hole in my tooth, but I still refused to get in the chair. In the end, it took six dentist staff to hold me down so that the dentist could look in my mouth. I fought and fought before I tired and gave up the fight. The appointment was not as bad as I had thought it would be, but they said that I had to come back for a filling and tooth extraction. As soon as we got outside of the dentist building, my mother slapped my legs and told me how ashamed she was of me.

Forgiveness: The Journey to Healing the Heart

She said, 'Look at your younger brother and sister, how they behaved themselves, and yuh ah big gal behaving like that.' The second time at the dentist was worse than the first time.

This time it was just me and my mother, and I had received a stern warning from her. She had the belt in her bag and was ready to use it. So I politely sat in the dentist chair. I had made my mind up to comply with them, but when I saw the dentist with a needle, that was all it took. The fight was on. This time the dentist staff were all ready for me. But they needn't have worried. My mum took the belt out of the bag and showed it to me. I froze, they gave me the needle, and I was out cold. When I came around, they had pulled out the tooth with the hole.

One day my mum and I went to Woolworth's on Soho Road to do some shopping. My mum saw Mrs. Drysdale. I was so happy to see her. My mum and Ivy exchanged pleasantries, and she told mum that she and her family had moved to the other side of Handsworth Park. I was excited. It was closer to my house, and she told me to come and visit her any time I wanted. Whenever I was sent to Park Gate shops to buy anything for my mother, I would visit my adopted brother and mother, Donavan and Mrs. Drysdale. This continued for many years. Even when my mother beat me - which was quite often. I would run away to Mrs. Drysdale's house. I would cry and tell her what had happened and show her the marks all over my body. She would calm me down and give me a drink and some cake. She also made the best fried dumplins.

Audreia Josephs

Then she would advise me to try to keep out of my mother's way and to behave and do as I was told, to avoid any injury.

One day my mum went out with Miles and Mary and left me to clean and sweep the house. I was worried that I wouldn't get it right. I could never seem to do anything right, and whenever she had taught me to do anything, it was taught with a belt. I lived in constant fear of doing anything and everything wrong. Now here I was trying to clean and sweep up with no supervision. There was a knock on the door. I opened the door, and it was Auntie Cassie. She had come to see my mother. I told her that mum was out and that I didn't know what time she would be back. Auntie Cassie came in and sat down. While I was doing my chores, she spoke to me. She asked me how I was doing at school with a genuine interest in my wellbeing. She was one of the few adults who spoke to me and not at me. She saw how I was holding the handle of the broom and gently said to me, 'Audrey, your sweeping would be easier if you pushed the broom forwards instead of pulling it behind you.' She gently took the broom from my hands and demonstrated. I had never thought of that. My mother had never said that to me. My Auntie Cassie was the very first person who taught me with love. I had always loved my Auntie Cassie, but I loved her even more after that day. It was a life lesson that I carry even today.

We continued to rent out the upstairs half of our house. There was a nice lady living upstairs called Monica who had two young sons who were about the same age of my younger brother and sister. Her

Forgiveness: The Journey to Healing the Heart

husband was a bit surly, but Monica was a very glamorous and friendly young woman. She used to let me come upstairs in her bedroom to watch her put her make up on. Monica fit well into the 1970s with her afro wigs and afro puffs and miniskirts. She looked like Diana Ross. There was another lady called Donna who lived upstairs with her two sons. She was also a very kind lady. I felt very lucky to have Monica and Donna living upstairs. I was able to speak to them whenever I felt troubled. They both always had time for me. One day in a conversation with Monica, I found out that her birthday was close to mine in June. She asked, 'Have you ever had a birthday party?' I said no, I hadn't. She told me that she was going to arrange a birthday party for me. I could hardly sleep for the next two months. As it got closer and closer, I got more and more excited about the prospect of having my own birthday party. When June 21st 1971 arrived, Monica honoured her word and gave me my very first birthday. There was a birthday cake and all kinds of goodies and sweets on the table. I'm not sure who brought what, between Monica and my mum. It was a small party, attended by my family, a few of my cousins from next door, Donna and her sons, Monica and her children and, of course, my best friend Maureen. Monica brought her record player and some records down, and we had the party in our dining room. We danced to Marvin Gaye, Al Green, Isaac Hayes and Jackson 5. We danced, ate, sang and played games until we were tired. Even my mum had fun. It was one of the best days of my life.

Audreia Josephs

In the same year, my mother sent for my older twin brother and sister, Robert and Jane, in Jamaica. When my mum told me that my older brother and sister were coming to England, I was so excited. I tried to imagine how wonderful it was going to be to have a big sister. It would be nice to have a big brother, but I was more excited about meeting my big sister. I told my friend Maureen how everything would be perfect. Mum left me to care for Miles and Mary when she went to the airport to pick them up. She was gone for most of the day. She had left food for us, and I had fed Miles and Mary. However, soon we were feeling hungry again. We loved Ritz crackers, so I fed Miles, Mary and myself some Ritz crackers with jam. We really enjoyed them, but I didn't notice the crumbs from our feast that had fallen on the floor. Throughout the afternoon, we ran all around the house, grinding the biscuit crumbs more and more into the floor. When my mum returned with my older twin sister and brother, she took one look at the state of the house and beat me in front of my freshly arrived sister and brother.

As the weeks passed, I tried to be friendly with my newly arrived older brother and sister, but they were not very friendly with me in return. They did not smile. They mainly only spoke to each other. I had been the eldest before they came to the UK. Now I had to get used to being a younger sister.

I had thought that life was going to be great once they arrived. I had thought that having an older brother and sister would make me

Forgiveness: The Journey to Healing the Heart

feel safe, that if anyone picked on me they would defend me. Little did I know that they would become a part of my sadness? Jane in particular did not like me from day one, while my brother Robert was indifferent to me. Though Robert would take care of me later, it took a lot more for Jane to feel protective. In a way my mum conditioned her eldest children - as she had conditioned my extended family - to dislike me and to express it openly. Jane showed her dislike in everything she did towards me. She voiced how spoilt she thought we all were. In her head, we were over privileged, English-born kids. She knew nothing about my life or struggle. From the day they arrived, mum taught them how to treat me, and every so often my older brother and sister would beat me. I had gone from one person beating me to now three. I hated every single one of them. My two older siblings both seemed to find me a joke. No matter what I did, they laughed at me. I used to call mum 'mother', and they thought that that was funny. They would say, 'Nuh kill mi wid yuh English, Miss English.' I started speaking with a Jamaican accent to avoid being laughed at, but my Jamaican accent angered my mum; she wanted us to have a clear-sounding use of the English language. She would tell Jane and Robert that they had spoilt my English accent. 'Listen how Audrey talk bad now.' To hear me speak now, you might think that I was born in Jamaica, though I think that I have a hybrid Jamaican-Brummie-English accent. My Jamaican family finds it hard to believe that I was born in England with my accent. I have Jane and Robert to thank for that. As twins, they tended to keep

Audreia Josephs

themselves to themselves to the exclusion of everyone else. Here were another set of people that had their own kind of silent code. I felt entirely left out of this family and with no way of getting in. I still had no idea that my eldest sister Gen and brother Jim were my full sister and brother, that we had the same mother and father. If I had known that, maybe I would not have felt so alone and on my own. I was a majority not a minority; there were three of us. If had known about all of these things, I would have felt more empowered. All my mother had said to me while I was growing up was that I had brothers and sisters in Jamaica. One day I saw a picture of my eldest sister Gen. I looked and looked at the picture. I thought, 'I don't remember taking this picture.' I actually thought that it was a picture of me. I was staring at a face that looked exactly like my own. The girl even had hair short like mine. My mum saw the puzzled look on my face and said, 'Fool ah yuh sister.' I could not take my eyes of off that picture. I thought, 'There's someone else in the world that looks like me. Is she having a horrible life like me?' My father had brought my mum to England. My dancing effort money had paid the deposit on the house in which I had been abused and beaten. I was treated like I was nothing. I knew that I deserved better. There was always a voice inside saying, 'Be strong.' But over the years, I would struggle with maintaining my strength while facing everything life kept throwing at me.

    In 1971 I was ten years old. I had steadily been doing Art for two years and knew that I was good at it. Even my teacher had commented

Forgiveness: The Journey to Healing the Heart

on how good my work was. I was soon due to leave Farm Street to attend a secondary school. Someone from an Art school came to visit and speak to us about the Art school and said that those of us who were good enough might obtain a scholarship to attend. We were each given a letter and an application form. I was so excited. I was not very good at many things, but I knew that I excelled in drawing and painting. I told my friend Maureen that I would be going to Art school. That day when my mum got home from work, I didn't even wait for her to take off her coat before proudly showing her the letter and application form. I asked her to fill them in. She said yes. I thought, 'This is the best day of my life.' A few days later my mother came to the school. I was in class and was told that my mother was outside. I proudly went out to my mum. She had come to see the headmistress Mrs. Gower to discuss me going to Art school. Mrs. Gower had been in a meeting, so my mother had to see the deputy head instead. My mum said to him, 'Audrey says that she can go to Art school, so I have brought in the forms.' The deputy head said to my mother, 'She is not good enough to go to Art school.' I said to my mum, 'No, mummy, he is not my Art teacher. He does not know anything about my work. Please speak to my Art teacher.' But the deputy head again said, 'Mrs. Henry she will not be going to art school because she is not good enough.' My mum looked at me and said, 'Him say yuh not good enough,' and just like that my mother turned and left the school. I crumpled into floods of tears. No one could console me. When my mum got home

Audreia Josephs

from work, I pleaded with her to come back to school and speak to my Art teacher. All I got back was 'Dem say yuh not good enough.' Every time I heard the words not good enough, I felt broken. Another man's words were more powerful than mine. My mum had let me down by believing that my dreams and me were not worth fight for. The school had let me down inspiring and then crushing my dreams. **I wore the coat of not-good-enough for many years after that day. I carried it into every area and relationship in my life. I felt robbed of my dreams. I became a closet artist. I never stopped painting or drawing, but I hardly ever showed my work to anyone. Not many people knew or know that I am an artist. Some people who have known me for a very long time will probably be surprised.** There were other children whose parents had filled in the form, and a few of them were given the opportunity and scholarship to attend Art school. When I saw other children given the opportunity to go, my heart sank. There was only one girl among the group whose work I thought was better than mine. She was a mixed race girl called Cleo. None of the other chosen children's work was better than mine. What I also noticed was that with the exception of Cleo all of the chosen children were white, with not one black child among them.

    Robert and Jane were too old to go to school - seventeen years old - when they came to England, so my mum found them jobs in the local curry patty factory. Everybody in the area went to this curry patty shop. They even sold patties out of town to places like London, Leeds

Forgiveness: The Journey to Healing the Heart

and Manchester. I had first met Mrs. Edwards when I was six years old, when I was still attending Grove Lane School. At the time they had owned a dress making shop on the corner of Mostyn Road and Grove Lane, just in front of my old school. One day while traveling on the open top number 70 bus near her shop, I fell off and hurt my face. I was taken to Mrs. Edwards shop to wait for the ambulance. She had seen what had happened. Her husband was also family to my mother. Now Robert and Jane were working for them. I had to pass the curry patty shop every day on my way to school. Mrs. Edwards was always happy to see me and would offer me a curry patty. Sometimes she would say, 'Go around the back to the factory and get your brother Robert or sister Jane to give you a patty.' It turned out that Mrs. Edwards had a famous daughter, Rustie Lee. This became a regular routine after school. Miles, Mary, Maureen and I and sometimes Maureen's younger brothers and sisters would all go eat our curry patties. The shop was on Soho Hill was called Gees Patty Shop.

Audreia Josephs

CHAPTER 4
School Life

Between 1971 and 1972, my mother met a man. His name was John 'Neckep' Smith. He came in our lives like a whirlwind, all smiles and nice words. I had seen him at some of the family neighbourhood parties. He was a name about town. You heard of him before you saw him. He was also a tall man; my mum seemed to like very tall men. He smoked cigars, and he had a face that reminded me of the actor 'John Wayne'. It turned out that 'John Wayne' was his favourite actor. He was missing a part of the top of his ear. We later found out that his ear had been bitten off in a fight during a domino match. This was way before Mike Tyson had done the same thing to Evander Holyfield. After that, everyone started calling him John 'Neckep'. We also found out that his pearly white teeth were all false. The story was that when he was a young man in Jamaica, all of his friends had had false teeth, and so he had wanted false teeth, too. He found a dentist to take out all of his good teeth that he could have false teeth like everyone else.

He was also Auntie Sweetie's cousin and Auntie Gertie's brother. He asked Miles, Mary and I what we would like. I said shoes, and he

Forgiveness: The Journey to Healing the Heart

said that he would give our mother the money to buy them. When we got the shoes, I promptly announced that we were going to call John Smith, 'Dad'. Deep down in my heart, I wanted my dad, and I just had to try and fill that hole with someone else. Soon Mr. John 'Neckep' asked my mother to marry him, and finally my mum was going to be a Mrs. I was measured up for my flower girl dress. My siblings and I were all going to be a part of this wedding. Before I knew it, it was almost time for the wedding. My Auntie Sweetie was a very creative woman and used to do hairdressing. I was sent next door to get my hair done for the wedding. I thought, 'What hair???' My mum wanted me to look more like a girl, as opposed to the boy that I looked like. My auntie had a plan. I spotted all of this false hair lying around. 'Come in, Audrey, and sit down.' She proceeded to sew and pin hair on my very short hair. This went on for what seemed like hours. She continued pinning and curling coarse fake hair that scratched the back of my neck. When she had finished working her magic, she told me to take a look in the mirror. I was shocked. I had always wanted hair, but not like this. I had been given a beehive. It was heavy, and I looked strange, nothing like an eleven-year-old girl. I started crying. I said, 'Everybody is going to laugh at me.' 'Nobody is going to laugh at you,' Auntie said. This was not the first time that they had done this to me. I had attended another family member's wedding the year before, and Auntie Sweetie had pinned a hair piece to my head. They had not let me take it off and had sent me to school in it. When I had gotten to school, one of

Audreia Josephs

the boys had pulled it off of my head and used it as a football. I had punched him in the face, and as usual in my case, there had been a big fight. Now here they were doing it all over again to me. By the time I got down the stairs, I ran back to my house, only next door, just in case the children from the neighbourhood saw me. My little brother Miles saw the hair first. 'Is that you Audrey?' my seven-year-old brother asked. Miles was a bit more sensitive to my feelings than the others and did not laugh as much at me. But when my older brother Robert saw the beehive hair, he laughed and laughed. It was funny to him. He had previously taken to calling me dry head gal. Jane started laughing as well. I thought, 'What she is laughing at?' Her hair didn't look much better. Auntie had done her hair as well, and she was currently wearing large ringlets. Mary didn't say anything, but she didn't often say much. Mum said it looked good. I did not want to leave the house, but I had no choice. I was sent to the shop to buy something for Robert.

I was always being sent to the shop for something. Jane and Robert had jobs, which meant they also had money. Sometimes they would send me to the shop 10 times in one day. My mother did not like this and asked why they couldn't get a list together before sending me to the shop over and over again. I knew that they were using me, but it got me out of the house, so I was kind of okay with it. I would always take my time to get back home after they sent me out. They would ask me to buy pop, biscuits or other goodies. I would bring the items back to them, but they never shared these things with me. On

Forgiveness: The Journey to Healing the Heart

this occasion when I was sent to the shop, I think it was more for their own entertainment. I decided to take Miles and Mary with me. When I walked past my friend Valerie's house, she came out and saw my new beehive hair style. She was sympathetic as she, too, had short hair like mine. I told her how much I hated the new hair, but because of this wedding I had to keep it on. At least this was all taking place during my seven week school holidays. I wouldn't have to start my new school with this bee-hive hair style. The closest shop to us was a newsagent and a sweet shop and was not far from the corner of Ivy Road and Soho Road. They had all kinds of sweets like lemon bon bon's, rhubarb, custard, barley sugar, toffee of all kinds, spaceship sweets, lemon sherbet. I could have stood in that shop all day given half a chance. The shop also sold cigarettes. I had always been sent to the shop. Mr. Slick used to do it, too. He smoked Capstan cigarettes. Then when John 'Neckep' came, I would go and get him 5 Hamlet cigars.

The day of my mum and John 'Neckep' Smith's wedding came. The wedding took place during our seven week school holidays. No one in the area had ever seen anything like it. Auntie Sweetie had also done my mother's hair, and with all that hair she looked like Tina Turner. Every one put their dresses on. The flower girls had deep pink velvet dresses, and the bridesmaids had light blue satin dresses. The bridesmaids put their make up on first, and then it was my turn to laugh at my older sister Jane. Monica was one of the bridesmaids. She had put light blue eyeshadow on Jane, which was meant to match the

Audreia Josephs

dresses. It did not, however, complement her dark skin, and I silently laughed. Jane was cussin about the make-up. I found it so funny. There were twelve bridesmaids and twelve flower girls. The ceremony took place at the Methodist Church on Rookery Road, and the reception took place at James Watt School on Bolton Road. When the reception ended at the school, it was on to Whitehall Road. Some of my older male cousins - Auntie Cassie's sons; my older cousin Terry looked like Smokey Robinson, and Andy and Blake looked like the boys from The Jackson 5 - were into sound systems and had strung up the giant speaker boxes and music between the two houses. The kids had pulled down the garden fence between our garden and next doors' garden to make one enormous garden. My cousins and I ran through the garden, from house to house. My uncle had done the cooking with my mum's help. My Auntie Sweetie had baked cakes. My family were all excellent cooks, real party cooks. They cooked in the largest pots that I have ever seen. Curry goat, fried chicken, Manish water, and saltfish fritters were just a few of the dishes that kept coming out of the kitchen nonstop. The wedding party lasted for one solid week. Every day was a party day. Not even a royal wedding party lasted one week! These were some real party people. We joined the grown-ups in the partying. There were too many cousins to count. When it got very late all the kids were sent upstairs to bed. We turned the floor into a big bed and all slept on the floor together, but we all decided that we wanted the kids' party to continue. I volunteered to get the drinks, and someone

Forgiveness: The Journey to Healing the Heart

else would have to get the food. The plan was that I would sneak into the kitchen, on the pretext that I was getting water, to get us kids some strong drinks. The grown-ups were having too much fun to even notice that I was helping myself to drinks. My favourites were Cherry B. Babycham, and Snowball. My cousins and I danced, ate fried chicken and dumpling, drank, and made up our own words to the songs that were played. We did this every night for a week. Some of us ate and drank too much and were sick the next day. Our parents never guessed that we were having a nightly kids' party. We took turns guarding the top of the stairs on the lookout for grown-ups. Whenever a grown-up came to check on us, we would all pretend to be asleep

The one week wedding reception party turned out to be very lucrative for me. In the 60s and 70s, you could get refunds for empty glass drink bottles. This is where being an entrepreneur came in. I had done it before on a small scale; it had only been one or two bottles here and there. But this was much larger. I got garbage bags, and I went around both houses every day that week and picked up bottles. The grown-ups thought that I was cleaning up. I was, but not in the way they thought. I made several trips to Miss Knight's shop at Park Gate. 'Where you get so many bottles from?' she asked me. She was giving me pounds instead of the usual pence. Miss Knight was a Jamaican-Chinese lady. She had two shops, one on Thornhill Road by Park gate and the other on Soho Road by Grove Lane. Miss. Knight asked too many questions. Time to change shops. Every time I got the bottle money, I bought sweets. I even bought sweets for my friend Maureen. I also bought a Bunty magazine. I shared the sweets with Miles, Mary and some of my cousins.

This was the year that I was meant to be going to secondary school. Since I did not get in to Art school, I would be going to one of the local schools. I wanted to go to Handsworth Wood Girls School. Most of my friends would be going to that school. So I asked my mum if I would be able to go to that school as well? Because we lived next door to our family, the grown-ups had a way of speaking to each other from window to window. One day I overheard my Auntie Sweetie say to my mum, 'I wouldn't let Audrey go to Handsworth Wood Girls School because the boys' school is next door, and they all end up in Handsworth Park after school. Pure man and woman,' meaning that she thought that they were having sex in the park. My mother then decided to send me to Handsworth New Road Girls' School. Auntie then promptly sent her son Rocky, who was the same age as I was, to Handsworth Wood Boys' School. I was sad at first, but was overjoyed when I found out that my best friend Maureen's mum, was sending Maureen to the same school. A few of my other friends from Farm Street would also be attending Handsworth New Road. The year we left Farm Street School, they knocked the school down. There was a new school being built near our home on Welford Road to be called Welford Road Junior and Infants. My younger brother and sister would be attending that school.

Forgiveness: The Journey to Healing the Heart

My first day at Handsworth New Road Girls in September 1972 was memorable, for many reasons. Dressed in our new school uniforms - navy blue pleated skirts, navy blue jumpers, white blouses, blue and yellow stripped ties, white socks and black shoes - we all had to attend assembly. Our headmistress Miss Read wore her hair in two plaits pinned to her head. She looked a bit like Princess Leia in Star Wars. She gave us a long speech about what was expected of us and how we were to behave in a girls' school. We were all assigned classes. I was so happy when Maureen ended up in the same class as I did. Our class teacher introduced herself to us. Her name was Miss Bear. I liked Miss. Bear the moment that I met her. She was very gentle. We were meant to be writing something about a time table. I thought, 'Oh no I'm not any good at my times table,' and started to worry. I did not understand that we were meant to be writing out our class weekly schedule. The next thing I found out was that all of our lessons would not take place in the same classroom. In junior school, almost every lesson we had was in the same classroom. Now here we were being told that we would have to go here and there and find our own way around to each lesson. We were also told where we could and could not walk and in which direction. Some of the teachers walked around in gowns and mortarboard hats, very much like the teachers in the Harry Potter films.

    Our class was 1.2. 1.1 was for the bright children; 1.2 and 1.3 were for average children. I followed all the other girls to our classes. We

Audreia Josephs

found ourselves in a large classroom for English language class. At the desks in an insert, there was an inkwell, a small container with ink in it. We were meant to use an ink nib - dip it into the ink and write with it. We were all just coming from junior school and had never seen an inkwell before. Our teacher had not yet come in to the classroom, and we were all laughing and playing around with the ink when suddenly a fight broke out. Ink was thrown all around the classroom. Someone threw ink in a girl name Valerie's face. Valerie's eye was blue from the ink. Valerie was just about to give a girl a beat down when the door suddenly opened. There stood our English language teacher. 'What's going on here?' he shouted. We all froze on the spot. Valerie was sent to get cleaned up, and we were told to clean up our classroom. The teacher walked to the front of the classroom and announced his name - Mr. Niven. We all got detention on our very first day. What an introduction to our English teacher and our new school. It was only our first day, and class 1.2 was already famous.

    I only liked going to school to get away from my family and to see my school friends. It was a form of escapism, even when I was getting in trouble. Learning was hard, as I had left junior school with less than a basic knowledge of reading and writing. In secondary school, I was introduced to Home Economics. The only part of that class I enjoyed was the cooking and baking; I had loved baking since I was eight years old.

    Things changed even more at home now that my mum and

Forgiveness: The Journey to Healing the Heart

John 'Neckep' were married. Suddenly everything centred on him. He liked butter beans. I was okay with eating them at first, but when they started making daily appearances in almost every meal, I started complaining. I told her that she was spoiling our meals as no one liked them. If I didn't like something, I was not shy in being vocal about it, even if it meant receiving a slap in the mouth. My mum used to say to me, 'Why do you have to be a mouth for everybody?' But all of my favourite meals were spoilt. I hated butter beans to the point that for years later, you could not even say the word butter beans around me. It's now a running family joke. They say butter beans and wait to see my facial expression. But my mum had to keep her man satisfied, even if it meant disappointing and upsetting her children. My stepfather used to walk in the house, go into the kitchen, watch my mum dishing up his dinner, turn and walk out of the kitchen, go upstairs, take a seat and wait for my mother to carry his food up to him on a tray. I used to think, 'Why can't he carry his own food up with him?' No man would ever make me feel subservient to him. I saw my mother as weak, catering to a man's needs. When she had finished serving him, she would grab a bowl, put her own food in it and eat with her spoon. No fancy gold-rimmed trays or napkin. As young as I was, I found all of that distasteful and disrespectful. I made a vow that no man was ever going to treat me like that.

John 'Neckep' was the kind of person who did everything on a large, loud scale. He would host parties, even if it meant using all of the

Audreia Josephs

household money. He always had to put on a show. At times he partied away our pocket money. Whenever his family or friends came from out of town to visit or just turned up, it was game on and nonstop drinks.

My beatings did not stop. I was pounced on for any infractions. As I got older my mother's style of beatings changed. I was now beaten with electric wire cords or anything else she could get her hands on. My mum also became aware that I had become lightning fast and could dodge the belt faster than she could move it. So she took to holding me down, pinning me on the ground and putting her foot, knee or hand around my neck, and using her free hand to beat me. I think that she must have learnt some of those moves for the wrestling that we use to watch on a Saturday. She never treated Miles and Mary like this. In fact she hardly ever slapped them. My family was happy to put the word out to everyone that I was bad and mad. It was easier for them to do that than it was for them to admit that I was an abused child. My Jamaican family did not know me but somehow still got a twisted impression of me, coming from the information that they were fed. It hurt that they had formed an opinion of me without getting to know me, but how could know me when we lived on different continents? They were missing important information, like of how badly I was treated here in the UK. I used to hear my mother discussing me with some of the family or her friends about how she held me down and beat me. She would tell anyone who would care to listen to her. She would go into graphic details. At times I would hear the delight in her

Forgiveness: The Journey to Healing the Heart

voice, as if she was justified in treating me this way. She sounded as if someone had given her a gold medal for her whipping and beating skills, no shame in her voice about it at all. Somehow it must have made her feel in charge and powerful. She had no idea that every time she did that to me that it opened old wounds. She poured insult on top my injury. She even did it in front of my husband and me, when I was in my 40s, as if it was some sort of entertaining family story. It was such a mortifying experience. In that moment she would break down years of work that I had done with myself.

Mother became pregnant with John 'Neckep's baby. I'm not sure what happened, but during her pregnancy it never took much for her to attack me. She would come after me with belt in hand and big belly in tow. I looked at her and thought, 'Is she mad?' I ran and grabbed the paraffin heater, which was not on, and held it over my head, telling her that if she came any closer to me I would throw it on her. I stood breathing fast and defiantly stared her in the eyes, daring her to hit me. She must have seen the fire in my eleven-year-old eyes, or maybe she was considering her own pregnant state. But she backed off and walked away. It felt like a little victory. Little did I know that she would store this against me for later, saving this missed beating for another day.

My new baby sister Jade was born on the 8th of March in 1973. My mum had neglected to inform the hospital that she had 3 other children in Jamaica; she had only told them about the five of us that were in the UK. She had been trying to keep up appearances, but little did she know that that could endanger her life! She had decided that she would have a home birth, and there were complications. My sister came in weighing more than nine pounds, and she had to have her collarbone broken in order to be born. My mum haemorrhaged and needed an immediate blood transfusion. To make things even more complicated, she is in a rare blood group and needed to be airlifted by helicopter to a specialist hospital. Mum and Jade survived the whole event, and they were back home a week later. The midwife who saved my mother's life was my junior school friend Diane's mother, Mrs. Broomfield.

Meanwhile at school, class 1.2 got into trouble on a daily basis. As a class, we were an exception to the rule. As an all girls' school, our headmistress Miss Read thought that it was her job to refine us and turn us into young ladies. But our class was having none of it. We talked loudly, laughed loudly and joked in class. We even sang loudly. There was a singing group at the time called 15,16 & 17. We sang all of their songs in school. We were just loud in about everything. All the teachers heard about class 1.2 and were always ready for us.

Mr. Niven never took to us after the ink fight. If we laughed or spoke during his class, he would throw a piece of chalk at us. One day he threw the chalk at me, and I promptly threw it back at him. I was sent to stand outside of the class. That was the beginning of my hallway learning. I was always being sent out to stand in the hallway or to the head's office. Some of the teachers displayed a dislike for us or were racist toward us. We gave those teachers that we knew that did not like us or who we knew were racist a hard time. We would speak in Patois or back slang, just so they wouldn't understand what we were saying to each other. We would tell jokes to each other, or just kiss our teeth, push up our mouths and roll our eyes.

    My love affair with reading started during my first year at Handsworth New Road School. Our English literature teacher was called Miss Rawlingson. Miss Rawlingson was also the deputy head of the school. She was a tall thin woman with a pageboy hair style. She was very stern and hardy ever smiled. In Miss Rawlingson's class, we were each given books from which each student read a paragraph. Miss Rawlingson began the reading, and then we were meant to continue. I hated when it came to my turn. I did not like reading out loud. I would stutter, and my mouth would get dry. I was not able to read very well and lacked confidence in it. One day Miss Rawlingson gave us a book called Heidi by Johanna Spyri. This book was about a young girl growing up in the Swiss Alps. I was very intrigued by all the characters in the book. I even looked forward to attending Miss Rawlingson's class just so that I could hear the next part of the story. It was like discovering a whole new world. I became aware that I was using my imagination. I could see all of the characters in my head. For the very first time, a book took on a life of its own for me. I was disappointed when we finished the book. So I started going to the

Audreia Josephs

library to get reading books for myself instead of cooking books. I loved the books that I read so much that I would not bring them back to the library and then had to pay fines for not returning them.

The end of the school year came very quickly, and we were all given our school report. My report was very glowing. I was very surprised reading it. Most of my earlier reports had stated things like, 'Audrey must try harder.' Now here I was reading that I was an exemplary student. I thought, 'They must be speaking about someone else.'

It turned out that they were. The other Audrey Henry - remember Yvonne's older sister? - attended the same school. She was four years older than I was. When I looked at the class year on the report, I realised that they had given me the wrong one. I went to find the other Audrey, and I told her what had happened. By now she had been given my school report and had known instantly that it was not hers. To this day we still laugh about our mixed up school reports.

The year after I started Handsworth New Road School, the powers that be - also known as the government - decided to mix our school with the boys' school next door. We had a new headmaster. The transition from a girls' school to mixed was hard. We did not want to sit next to the boys in class. We stood on one side of the playground, and they stood on the other side. Some of the girls already knew some of the boys. Our classes changed as well. We were now called class 2.2, and our class was now no longer in the main school building. We had to walk 15 to 20 minutes to the annex on Bacchus Road. Sometimes we

Forgiveness: The Journey to Healing the Heart

had to walk back to the main school for some of our lessons, even in the freezing cold or snow. Sometimes I would walk very slowly to the main building. 'Where were you, Audrey?' 'I was coming up from the annex, Sir.' 'How come the other children got here before you?' 'I don't know, Sir. They must have ran, plus I had to go to the toilet,' I would answer with a big smirk on my face. 'Class has already started. Get out and stand in the hallway.' 'Okay.'

I was in that school for five years, and I think that I spent at least three of those years standing in the hallway for punishment, on litter duty or in the Headmasters office. I had a hard enough time learning Maths, and soon they introduced Algebra. ALGEBRA? I had just about grasped numbers, and now they added letters and Greek words. I thought, 'That's it! Here I come, hallway. Just give me the detention now.' This was my giving up energy. I didn't even try to learn Algebra. I also had a problem with learning English history. I could not relate to the Roundheads or the Cavaliers. King Henry meant nothing to me except a shared name. I never saw myself or black people in what they were teaching us. People might think that just because we British Blacks were born in the UK that we were considered English, and that we would be well up on British history. But we were trying to find our own identity. We were not accepted, and most of us did not accept their British history because their history showed us as slaves and servants. We were not Jamaican or Caribbean. We were not English. We were told that we were British citizens, meaning that our parents

Audreia Josephs

were not born here. Whenever we encountered a Caribbean person or went to Jamaica, we were told that we were English. A lot of Caribbean people seem to think that because we were born in the UK that we have been given some type of extra privileges. What a lot of people did not understand, was that we were black children, and we were viewed and treated that way. That left us confused.

My mother had taken to buying our clothes from the church jumble sales. She found every jumble sale in Birmingham. I was the one that was expected to accompany her on these trips. She expected me to be in the dig, digging through old clothes and finding the best items. I hated doing it, especially when the sale was in our local area. I felt ashamed and worried that people I knew might see us queuing up to get in. I used to turn my head away from my mother and act as if I was not with her. That kind of behaviour got her mad. She would start on about my father and how he wasn't giving her a penny for me. She would go on and on.

By the time I was thirteen years old, I was expected to do so many things. We had a man that used to deliver the paraffin weekly. If the paraffin ran out, I was expected to take an old pushchair, place the three-gallon oil pan in it and wheel it up to Soho Road, where there was a small petrol station next to Piers Road. I would be given the money to fill the paraffin can, and I would then wheel the filled can back home. I also had to do the same for the dirty clothes. The launderette, or 'bag wash' as we called it, was just across the road

Forgiveness: The Journey to Healing the Heart

from the Elite cinema on Soho Road. I spent many hours watching the machine go around and around. I was always able to keep warm, with all the dryers going at the same time. Sometimes the launderette was so full of other people that it could take hours to do the washing. All the local families used it. Sometimes doing the laundry was a great escape from the rest of my family. I would see some school friends or other friends from the area. But I hated anyone seeing me with that broken down old pushchair. Sometimes I would put the clothes in the washing and disappear off to the park to play with my friends or just get lost in my own space. I would get so lost in my day that at times I would forget the time and would end up running back to the laundry. By the time I returned, the assistant would have taken my laundry out of the machine and placed it in baskets. Then I would have to wait in the queue for the dryer, and I could end up spending up to four hours in the launderette. Sometimes someone from my family would come looking for me. My cousin Sharon would often come looking for me. She was one of Auntie Sweetie's daughters. She was supportive and very helpful, and she would help me to fold all of the clothes. I would also help her if she had any of her own washing to do. Sharon knew about my life, and I knew what her life was like.

    Sharon was one year older than I was. She and her brother Rocky had come to the UK from Jamaica in the early 1970s. She was a marvel to me. She could cook like a grown-up from a very young age. She said that they had given her a box to stand on and had taught her how to

Audreia Josephs

cook at the age of five; she was very skilful in the kitchen. She could also wash clothes with her hands. To see my cousin wash clothes, you would have thought that she was an adult. She could plait hair, and she even managed to plait my extra short hair. Sharon taught me how to plait with curtains. She could also clean a house better than even most of the grown-ups I knew. I admired my cousin. Having arrived from Jamaica with all of her skills, she had some big expectations on her very young shoulders.

Forgiveness: The Journey to Healing the Heart

CHAPTER 5
Responsibility

I got my very first job around this time. I had gone to the newsagents near the corner of Villa and Soho Roads, right next to the chip shop. I went in and inquired if they had any paper rounds jobs that needed to be filled. I started the very next day. It was a very early start, but I was used to staying in bed a bit longer on the weekends. This job had me up at 5AM in the morning, when it was still dark. Add to the early start a very heavy stack, and it was even harder. I hated delivering papers to the houses that had dogs. Sometimes I could not find the houses that I was meant to be delivering the papers to. I got sacked after about two weeks. After that, I went and got a weekend job in Handsworth Market. I loved that job. I sold perfumes and scented candles in the market. Everybody who lived in the area came to that market; I always saw my friends, but I had to be on my best behaviour when they were around. It was a good job because I was able to buy a carved Cote La Mont perfumed candle for my mum for Christmas at a discount. I only had the job for a few months. After Christmas I got another Saturday job in a bra shop, on the corner of Grove Lane and Soho Road. I was to stack shelves, get the correct size

Audreia Josephs

for customers and sometimes serve. Almost every girl in the area and their mothers would come into that shop for their Playtex long line bras. The mothers and grandmothers would come in for their pantie girdle. At times I even got to see some of my friends. I had that job for about eight months until I was no longer needed.

    My mum would sometimes work overtime on a Saturday. Now that I was thirteen years old, I was given the job of going to the City Centre to buy the chicken and vegetables for Sunday dinner. There was a lovely family that lived four doors away from our house. The husband and wife were called Jack and Dolly, and they were one of the first interracial couples that I had ever met. He was white, and she was black. Jack was a butcher in the City Centre, and my mother always bought her chicken from him. So now I had instructions of what to get and where to go, and I did the shopping instead. I had gone shopping several times with mum, so I knew where her favourite shopping spots were. Money in hand, I went off on my shopping adventure. When I would get to Jack's shop, other staff often offered to serve me, but I always waited for Jack. He knew exactly what my mother brought. I couldn't get it wrong. Also Jack always gave me a discount, but that was information that I did not share with my mum. So after I had bought everything that was on the shopping list, I would have a bit of extra money to have some fun with. I would take my time, in no hurry to get back home. One day on a sunny Saturday afternoon, the fun fair was in town. I decided to do all of the shopping that I had

Forgiveness: The Journey to Healing the Heart

been told to do, and as always I had extra money. There was a ride at the fun fair called 'The Cage'. It would go high up in the air and spin around. I was very adventurous and asked the attendant to watch my bags while I went on the ride. While I was on the ride, I had forgotten that I had my mum's leftover change from the shopping in my pocket. I was enjoying myself thoroughly, but when the cage flipped and spun around in the air, all of the money that I had in my pocket fell out and hit the ground. I even lost my bus fare to get home. I could not retrieve it since I was still up in the air. I started to feel sick and panicked. 'Oh no, she's going to kill me,' I thought. I couldn't wait for the ride to end. When I finally got off the ride, I ran around looking for the money. I found of it, scattered all around the place, and I managed to get enough money to get home with some to spare. When I got home mum said, 'Where is my change from the shopping?' I gave her the few pence that I had managed to find. 'How come that's all you got?' I lied and said that the price of some of the things had gone up. I think that she was so preoccupied with something else that she accepted my excuse. I thought, 'Phew. So no loss of life today.'

I had also become responsible for cooking the Sunday family meals, and my job was long and tedious. Rice was only sold in very large sacks, and if you wanted to buy rice, you would have to scoop it out with a jug and place it in to brown paper bags and get it weighed in order to purchase it. We would buy however much we need from Charlie"s shop on Soho Road, which was also next door to my favourite

Audreia Josephs

sweet shop. Charlie was an Asian man, with a very large belly that he was always rubbing. We always called him 'Big Belly Charlie'. Every year that belly got bigger and bigger. But he was a very friendly man. He knew my family very well. In fact Charlie's house was next door to my school, and his son also attended my school. To this day our families remain friends.

Cooking Sunday dinner started on Saturday. I had to burn all the loose feathers off the chicken over the gas fire, chop up the chicken into pieces, wash the chicken in lemon and vinegar, season it and place in the refrigerator. My next job was to pick the peas. I would look through a bag of dried peas to see if any dirt or small stones were in it, and then I would wash them and then soak them in a bowl overnight. I also had to do the same with the rice.

Monica from upstairs was beaten up very badly by her husband, and my mother had taken charge of situation. She had physically moved Monica's husband from the house, but Monica was scared that he would return. So she decided to move out with her two sons. Who would have known that these two boys would grow up to be a part of one of the biggest musical groups that Birmingham would ever see?

Almost every time I went out with my mum, some old lady would look at me and say, 'Is it a boy or girl?' My mum would reply, 'Are you stupid? Can't you see that she is a girl?' One day Mum had enough of this and decided to get my ears pierced. She thought that earrings would solve the problem of determining whether I was a boy or a girl.

Forgiveness: The Journey to Healing the Heart

Back in the 1970s, only girls got their ears pierced. I felt proud that I was going to the City Centre with my mum to get my ears pierced. The shop was called Robert's Jewellers; it was next to C & A on Corporation Street. To this day, the owner's son Daniel and I are still friends. The shop is still open on the other side of the road. Daniel is now the owner.

Donna left shortly after Monica and her family did. My stepfather's sister Auntie Diane moved in with her three children. Auntie Diane's eldest daughter Pat was just a little bit younger than I was. The younger children were Eve and David. They were Miles' and Mary's ages.

In my family, we seemed to double up on the names. What made it even more complicated was the fact that we were living next door to each other. We had two Janes; one was my sister Jane, and the other was my cousin Jane who lived next door. My sister was older and was called Big Jane, or Auntie Enid Jane, while my cousin, the younger one, was called Little Jane. We also had two Roberts. One was my older brother, and the other was my cousin next door. So again they were called Big Robert and Little Robert. There were two Pats. One was my cousin next door, and the other was my cousin living upstairs in our house - Big Pat and Little Pat. We even had three Davids. One was my cousin next door, who we called White David, since he was very light-skinned. The other Danny was another cousin, living upstairs. He was called Black David or Auntie Diane's David. The third David - who

Audreia Josephs

was also a cousin but lived out of town - was called Big Out-of-Town David. He was as wide as he was tall. He was my stepfather's other sister Mertie's son. The grown-ups had not planned copy each other's children's names. In fact most of the children had been born before they had even known each other. We loved each other, and meant no offence to each other with our 'white' and 'black' nicknames. These were just our expressions to and for each other. Now that I'm a grown-up, I feel a bit embarrassed that those were the terms that we used for each other.

Around the same time that Auntie Diane arrived, we got new neighbours on the other side of our house as well, the Greens and the Halls. Both families were equally nice. The house next door was set up very much like our house. It had become flats but had separate front doors. The flat downstairs housed a husband, wife and two very young children, and the upstairs flat housed a husband, wife, four sons and one daughter. Belinda and her brothers went to the same school as I did. Belinda was the only girl among four brothers, and she was only a year or two younger than I was. She was one of the kindest girls that I had ever met. We became friends. One day she invited me into her bedroom at her house. I had never seen a young girl's bedroom look the way Belinda's bedroom did. She had a dressing table full of perfumes and scented creams - Avon's Sweet honesty, the matching set, and Timeless perfume and cream. I stood staring. She said, 'Do you want to smell them? You can spray some on you if you want to.'

Forgiveness: The Journey to Healing the Heart

I said yes. She was so kind that after trying them, she offered to give me whichever perfumes I liked. 'Won't your mum be upset if you give away your perfumes?' I said. Belinda said, 'No, my mum will not mind.'

    In 1974, my mum went to America. She had secured a sponsor and went with the aim of securing a green card in order to obtain residency. She was in America for about nine months. Nine months of no beatings - no beatings from her anyway. While my mum was gone, she left Jane, Robert and my stepfather John 'Neckep' in charge of us. My stepfather loved to gamble and could often be found a few hundred yards down the road at an old gambling house between Whitehall Road and the corner of Broughton Road. The woman who owned the house was called Shirley. If not at the gambling house, he could be found at the Ivy House pub. Thus my stepfather often left us to our own devices. Jane and Robert were working, so they got on with their own lives and left us alone most often. One day Jane told Miles, Mary and me to clean up the house. We obviously didn't do it to her standard, and she came over to hit me. She was rarely nice to me. When she hit me, I grabbed her by the collar. She hadn't realised that I was now as tall as she was. We were eye to eye. She shouted to Robert, and he came in the dining room where we were standing and where I had been mopping the floor before she'd come in. I reached for the mop and went to push it into Robert's face. After that day, neither Jane or Robert ever tried to hit me again.

    One night while my mum was still in America, my stepfather

came back home from his gambling night out and had fallen asleep with a lit cigar. It fell in to Jade's cot while she was in it. Somehow my sister Jane managed to get Jade out of the cot before it was set ablaze and setting the rest of the house on fire. Jane always checked on our baby sister, and it was a good thing that she did. Jane and Robert raised the alarm. We all had to get up out of our beds, stand outside in our nightclothes and wait for the fire engine to come and put out the fire. When we were allowed back in to the house, everything smelt of smoke. The gas and electric had to be turned off, and we remained living like that in the house for the next seven months. Our only means of cooking and heating was from the paraffin heater. Jane and Robert did their best. They cooked corn beef and rice or pilchards and rice, but I was on paraffin duty again.

My stepfather John 'Neckep' and my sister, his daughter Jade, would always eat a very hearty meal every day, while the rest of us were left without. My Uncle Grant cooked for my stepfather - the two of them must have made some kind of arrangement - but he never once offered his niece and nephews even one grain of rice. My baby sister Jade started to get fat, while Miles, Mary and I were wasting away. It hurt to see how the uncle that I had once looked up to did not care or look out for us. He surely could see how we were living. No one would have ever believed that we were living in these kinds of conditions in England. Our mum was working in America and was sending over regular intervals of money for us, but somehow we never

Forgiveness: The Journey to Healing the Heart

saw any of this money. It was sent to our stepfather John 'Neckep'. At times we were so hungry, and it was hard to watch our younger sister Jade feasting on cakes, sweets, and ice cream in front of us. Our angel came in the form of our next door neighbour Mrs. Green. She used to look out of her window and if she saw us playing in the front garden, she would say to us, 'Would you like a dumpling?' I would say yes, and she would tell us to come up stairs to their flat. By the time we would get upstairs into the Greens' home, there would be three plates full of food. I loved Mrs. Green for her kindness. She saw how dirty and unkempt we were. I used to wish that she was my mother. Mrs. Green was a stunningly beautiful and well put together woman. Nothing ever out of place with her. There were times that I was so hungry that I used to go to Villa Road to my best friend Maureen's house to get food. We were inseparable. We did everything together. She knew so much about me. You would hardly have ever seen either of us without the other. We used to go to the chip shop on the corner of Villa Road and ask for scratchings. Scratchings came from the leftover batter from frying the fish. If we were lucky, we could also end up with a few stray chips. We loved this, as it was free, and they were only going to throw it away.

    I was now going through puberty, and my breasts popped out. I needed a bra. My mum was not here - she was still in America - and my sister Jane was unapproachable. One of Jane's friends called Marcia noticed my situation, and said to me, 'Audrey, I think you need a bra.'

Audreia Josephs

She offered to take me to the City Centre and buy me one. We went to the best bra shop in the city, and she bought me a beautiful pink bra. I was so happy. My first bra.

One day when I went to school, Mrs. Gray, the annex head teacher, stopped me. She was a very small lady, who spoke with an Italian accent. I thought that I was in trouble. She asked me to come to her office. When I got there, she told me to sit down. She was so gentle. She asked me if I was okay, and 'How are things at home?' I told her that my mum had gone to America. I told her all about the fire. I also told her that I was hungry. She gave me an apple, and then she asked me if I had an address for where my mum was living in America. I told her that I could get an address. She said that I should write and send a letter to my mum, that she would give me the postage stamp and post it for me. She told me to come to her office the next day and not to tell the other students why I was in her office. It took me three days to complete the letter. I was really proud of myself. I also sent one of my recent school pictures. I asked my mum why she had not sent me a present for my birthday, as it had been my birthday a few weeks earlier. Mrs. Gray posted the letter.

A few weeks later, my mum called us from America on Uncle Grant's telephone. At the time, uncle's house was the only house that had a telephone. She wanted to know why the collar on my school blouse was so dirty in my school picture. I had not even noticed that my collar was dirty. She also told me that she had sent money for my

Forgiveness: The Journey to Healing the Heart

birthday present because she knew that I wanted a cooking basket for school. She told me that she had sent my birthday money to my stepfather John 'Neckep'.

Mum came back from America very unhappy. She had not secured her green card. To this day, I am not sure if it was the letter that I had sent to her, my dirty shirt collar or the fire that nearly burnt our house down that had brought my mum back to the UK. Mum had brought clothes and gifts from America for us. I was given a nightdress and a bomber jacket. The jacket was a plum colour, with a white fur collar and lining. I was so excited. Our school disco would be in next few weeks, and I could wear them.

I had never been to any party outside of family ones. The day of our school disco came. Dressed in my burgundy maxi dress, and my bomber jacket, I couldn't do much with my hair, so I put a side part in it. I called for my friend Maureen and walked down St Michael's Hill, down towards Factory Road, down Benson Road, then Willis Road, over to Handsworth New Road and straight in to school.

Everybody looked differently out of school uniforms. We all stood in different groups, waiting for the music to start. The music was nothing like what we played at home. Bay City Roller's 'Shang ah lang', ABBA's 'Waterloo', Neil Diamond, Olivia Newton John. The black children just stood around with our arms folded. Some of the white girls were dancing with their arms all up in the air. I knew some of these songs because we all used to watch 'Top Of The Pops'. I used to

Audreia Josephs

watch it just in case a black group or singer came on. The teachers wanted us to dance. 'Aren't you going to dance, Audrey?' one of the teachers asked me. 'This music has not got any rhythm for me, Sirs,' I replied. The DJ then put on 'Kung Fu Fighting' by Carl Douglas. We all loved this song. We all started dancing and doing the bumps. The bumps was a dance where you bumped butts and hips with someone else. The boys did Kung Fu moves to the music. There were a few more records played that we all enjoyed. It was a good evening out.

Auntie Gertie became really ill and was rushed to hospital. She had osteoporosis, which used to be called brittle bone disease. My mother knew how close I was to Auntie Gertie and decided to take me to the hospital to visit her. When I walked in, I almost did not recognise her. She looked so small in that hospital bed. She didn't say much to me except that she hoped I was behaving myself. I had no idea that was going to be the last time that I would see her alive. Not long after my visit, Auntie Gertie died. I was allowed to take time off school to attend the funeral. The family held a big funeral for her. She was John 'Neckep's sister, so it was going to be a grand affair. I had never seen a dead person before. When they opened the casket for everyone to view the body, my curiosity got the better of me, and I walked up with everybody else. I looked at Auntie Gertie in that casket and held my breath. That was not my auntie in that box. It looked nothing like her to me. I wished I had not looked. That vision stayed in my head for some time. Before Auntie Gertie had died, she had left instruction for

Forgiveness: The Journey to Healing the Heart

certain items that should be given to family members. I found out that she had left her silver watch to my three-year-old baby sister Jade. She did not leave anything for me. I was hurt. We were close. She had known me a lot longer than she had known Jade. Then it hit me. I was not her real blood niece. Jade was her brother's child. No matter how close we were, we were not family. Auntie Gertie had sent me a clear message from the grave.

My little sister Jade was growing up very fast, too fast for a normal child. At three years old, she was the size of a five-year-old, plus she had a vocabulary that was shocking for a child of her age. When she started speaking, her words were pure swear words. She would say, 'Fuck off, you bastard,' at only two years old. Now we had no idea where she learned these words. I was blamed for Jade's dirty mouth. My family had never heard me swear, but they always blamed me if anything was wrong. My mother had taught them well. My baby sister Jade was about two years old when mum had left and gone to America. Jade did not know who mum was when she came back to England. Mum had left behind a baby and had returned to find Jade was a giant, overgrown toddler with the mouth to match. Jade's father John 'Neckep' let her get away with swearing. He let her get away with everything. My mum, however, wouldn't put up with any of it. The very first time she heard Jade swear, mum slapped her legs. Jade was in shock. No one had ever smacked her before. Jade stood frozen to the spot and wet herself. When Jade fully realised that she had been

Audreia Josephs

smacked for the very first time in her life, she went running straight to her dad to report mum. It was so funny I laughed until my belly hurt. I had waited a long time for the day to come when Miss Jade, the untouchable, got a real taste of mum's hand. John 'Neckep' did not take well to the fact that Jade had been slapped for swearing, and he argued with mum. It was many years later, when we were all grown up, that Jade told us that it was her father John 'Neckep' who had taught her to swear. He had thought it was entertaining to teach his baby daughter swear words. He also taught her how to drink white rum from a young age as well. She could - and can, if she chooses to - drink any man under the table.

    My stepfather John 'Neckep' had taken to calling any child in the house that was not his bastarding pickney. My mum's reply to him was, 'Leave me alone with my Joseph coat of many colours children,' meaning, leave me with my bastard children who have many fathers. I was disgusted with my mum for allowing him to call us those names. John 'Neckep's world centred around his daughter Jade. She could do no wrong. As she grew up, she would get anything she wanted, and if she didn't get it instantly, she would throw a big tantrum and create pure drama in the house. Jade would tell Miles, Mary and me, 'I can get anything I want. Just watch.' As soon as she heard the ice cream van playing his song, she would say watch. 'Dad, can I have an ice cream?' while she smiled that wicked smile at us. 'Yes, Jade.' No matter what he was doing, he would stop it, just to get her the ice cream. She would

Forgiveness: The Journey to Healing the Heart

run ahead of him, order whatever she wanted, then walk off, and he would pay for it. She would then walk proudly back into the house, smile and say, 'See?' Our stepfather never brought us an ice cream. I didn't mind not getting one because I was older, but I was upset about Miles and Mary not getting one. All of this was made even worse when Jade felt the need to have an ice cream every single time she heard an ice cream van outside. She became so popular with the ice cream vans that they started pulling up right outside of our house. If she wanted twenty ice creams, she could have them. Even when it made her sick, John 'Neckep' bought them for her, with never a one for Miles and Mary. I hated him for that. Jade had to be obeyed at all costs. I plotted thoughts of how I could kill her, my mother and stepfather.

  One day when I was left to babysit Jade, she wanted her own way as usual, so I stuffed an old sock into her mouth, just to shut her up. Then I hung her out of the top window. As soon as her father got home, she reported the incident. He grabbed me and pulled me in to in his and mother's bedroom and said to my mother, who was been sitting on the bed, that he was going to beat me. I thought, 'Is my mum just going to sit there and let this man beat me?' While holding my hands, John 'Neckep' grabbed the belt and swung it at me. I jumped back, and he missed. I pulled him towards the door. Somehow I had got one of my hands free. I got to the door and slammed it on his hand really hard. He dropped the belt, and I ran down the stairs, through the front door, which happened to be open, and ran up the road. I

Audreia Josephs

didn't come back home for hours. I went to the park and played on the slides and climbing frames. Later I went over to Mrs. Drysdale and got something to eat and then over to my best friend Maureen's to sit and chat on her door step. John 'Neckep' never tried to beat me ever again. I had damaged his hand. I later asked my mum why she just sat there watching him try to beat me. She said, 'I know that there was no way that he could beat you because you move swift and fast, and he wouldn't be able to hold you.' She should know, after all the years of beating me. She also knew that I was strong. I had had to be. It's a part of what saved me and my life from her clutches.

One day money had gone missing from my Uncle Grant's house next door. I had been over briefly that day to see my cousin Sharon. My uncle had heard that I had been over to his house and quickly assumed that I had stolen the money. At the time there were at least fifteen people living in that house, yet my name came out on top of the list of suspects. Mum told me that my uncle had sent word for me to come over to his house. I walked in smiling, saying, 'Yes, uncle?' He said that he had heard that I was in the house and that now money was missing. I told him that yes I had been to the house earlier in the day to see Sharon, but no I didn't take any money. He said, 'I think it's you, Miss Audrey.' He said that teef would have to pay somehow. He took the lid off a very large pot. It had boiling water in it. He told me to look inside of the pot. When I looked into the pot, there was a shiny 50p and nothing else. I was confused. I said to him, 'There is 50p in there.' He

Forgiveness: The Journey to Healing the Heart

said that 50p was the exact amount of money that had been stolen and that I should take it out of the pot of boiling water. I told him that I would not put my hand in a pot of boiling hot water. He said 'Teef must pay. Put yuh hand in and get the money out now.' I could not believe that my uncle was telling me to do this. I started to cry. He did not care about me crying. He grabbed my hand and tried to put it in the boiling water. I started to fight with him. I twisted and turned, got out of his lock hold and ran back next door to my house. After that day, I hated my uncle. He was as evil as his sister, my mother.

Audreia Josephs

CHAPTER 6
Wendnesfield

My father now once again decided to make an appearance. He knocked the door. My mum looked down at him from her upstairs bedroom window. 'Audrey, is yuh father,' she shouted. 'Go and open the door for him.' I ran and opened the door. I was faced by this tall dark stranger in a purple shirt. 'Do you know who I am?' he said to me. I said no. 'I am yuh fardha,' he said. I looked him up and down. By now, my mum and Jade were standing next to me at the front door. Mum invited him into her inner sanctum, the front room. I decided that I wasn't really that interested, so excused myself. I left them speaking, but then I heard mum call me back into the front room. 'Your father wants you to spend weekends at his house. Starting next weekend.' I was not given a choice. My father did not stay very long. My other brothers and sisters had seen my father in his tan-coloured suit and purple shirt and started laughing at his colour choices. Even my mother joined in with the laughing. 'Yuh fardah don't know how to dress.' The week rolled on, and before I knew it was the weekend. My father picked me up in a car. He was living in Wendnesfield. On the way to his house, he tried to make

Forgiveness: The Journey to Healing the Heart

conservation with me. 'You look like yuh mother,' he said. He was still a stranger to me, so I just looked out of the window. The drive seemed to take forever. Finally we got to his house, but it wasn't a house at all. It was an apartment. We walked upstairs, and he opened the door. He introduced me to his partner and his son Howard. 'This is yuh breadha,' my father said to me. Howard was two years younger than I was. I did not like him. This was the baby I had heard cry when my mother had dragged me to meet my father for the first time at two years old. I kept thinking, 'This boy's life looks perfect.' He had had our father all to himself all this time. 'This boy had better not breathe on me, or I might take his face off.' I had made up my mind that I was never going to like Howard, no matter what. I was shown to my room.

    My father was an excellent cook, and invited me in to the kitchen to watch and teach me how to make his Saturday soup. My only thought was that this is not why I am here. I had had enough of the standing in the kitchen, watching someone bark out instructions. My mum did it, and now here he was doing the same thing. I had an attitude. I stood with my arms folded, my left foot forward, rolling my eyes. 'This is how you peel a green banana,' he said. 'I already know,' I spat. My father added some of the most unusual ingredients to his soup. My mum never added some of the stuff that I saw my father add. He had a way of peeling a green banana that I had never seen. He was gentler than my mum. If she was trying to teach me how to do something in the kitchen, it usually came with a slap.

Audreia Josephs

My father's soup was the best soup in the world. After we had eaten, he took me to a warehouse that sold all kinds of household items. 'What do you need?' my father asked me I needed a new school jumper, so he got that for me. He also picked a large mustard-coloured suitcase. He said, 'You might need a suitcase,' and bought that as well. When we got back to his apartment, we all watched TV together. There was a programme that I always used to watch at home. As soon as my father left the room, I changed the TV station so that I could watch my show. My father came back into the room and said, 'Ah wah dis, pon de television?' I said Celebrity Squares. My father said, 'I don't care if ah silly battie squares, tun it over.' My father's partner was always kind and polite and gave me space with my father. She always referred to my father as Mr. Haughton. Later on in the evening, my father tried to have another conversation. He asked me what I would do if he hit me. I told him that I would hit him back. 'You would hit you father?' he asked. 'Yes I would,' I said, looking him straight in the eyes. I said to him, 'You haven't brought me up, so how do you think you could hit me?' 'Yuh cheeky like yuh mother,' he said to me.

My father's household went to bed early, so I had to go to bed at the same time. I was bored. I had brought my 'Jackie' magazine with me, so I read that. I must have fallen asleep with the light on because when I woke up, my father was standing in the doorway, staring at me. He said, 'Yuh know yuh ugly. Yuh look just like my brother.' I laughed. 'You are ugly, too,' I said back. We both laughed. He turned the light

Forgiveness: The Journey to Healing the Heart

off and closed the door. I hardly spoke to Howard during the whole weekend.

 I continued visiting my father on weekends for the next few months, but these visits would be short-lived. One weekend, he started talking about a song that he had written and was just about to record. I hadn't even known that my father could sing. So now I knew where my talent for singing came from. He played the song for me on his tape cassette machine. It was pretty good. In the song, my father addressed the unemployment and recession that Britain had been experiencing. For the next few weeks, all my father would talk about was his song. He had now been to the studio and had recorded it. One day he told me that his song was going to be played on the radio. At the time there was a popular reggae radio show hosted by Barry Curtis called Reggae Reggae. My father told me that his song would be played on the show in two weeks' time. I told all of my friends at school that my father's song would be played on the radio. Most of them did not believe me. Why would they? No one at school had ever even seen my father nor heard me talk about a father. The time came, and I listened to the show with my family. I was proud that my father's record was being played on air, and my family also seemed impressed. My mum just rolled her eyes and said that my father used to sing when they were in Jamaica.

 Once, however, my father and I came to a head and that would mean the end of our budding, amicable relationship. Whenever I went to spend the weekend with him, he always got me to do this and that

Audreia Josephs

for Howard. 'Go and make a cup of tea for Howard.' Or we would go out to visit one of his friends where he would show me off to everyone by saying 'Diss ah mi daughter.' (This is my daughter.) I really hated that. I thought to myself, 'How could he be boasting about a daughter that he really had not shown much interest in before now?' He had not made much contribution to my life. I was never really interested in visiting my father. Some of Auntie Sweetie's nephews and nieces lived about hundred yards away from my father's apartment. I found visiting father boring. My father was starting to make me feel like all he wanted was a slave for Howard. I was only too happy to disappear off up the road to my cousins. I would spend hours with them.

    Sometimes when I got back to my father's apartment, the family had all gone to bed, and I would have to knock on the door and wake everyone up. I only went back to my father's apartment to sleep. This did not go down well. 'I carry you here so that you can spend the weekend with us, and all you do is spend time up the road,' my father said. 'So?' I said. 'Every time I come here, you have me doing all kinds of stuff for Howard. This is Howard's house not mine, but you want me to serve him.' I had grudgingly spoken to Howard. I was really horrible to him. I had told him that the next time my father asks me to make him a cup of tea, I was going to poison and kill him by adding ground up glass. He must have told his mother or my father. My father said to me, 'You want to kill your brother? Don't come back to this house. Pack your things. I'm taking you back home.' I had not even been in

Forgiveness: The Journey to Healing the Heart

the house for twenty four hours, and now here I was, banished. I told my father that I didn't care if I came back to his home or not. I stood defiantly staring at him. He took me back home, and he told my mum what I had said to Howard and that I thought that I was a big woman. My mum laughed. She knew that sooner or later I would have given my father problems. She said to my father, 'You thought that she was going to move in with you, that is why you bought her that big suitcase.' She laughed in his face. My father left.

However for years afterward my father would come and visit his friend Dudley, who is also my baby sister Jade's godfather and who we all affectionately called 'teacher'. He lived about a hundred yards from our house on Ivy Road, around the corner. But though my father visited Dudley so near to my house, he never came to visit me. I had to pass Dudley's house to get to my friend Maureen's house. I went past that house nearly every day. On occasions my father would be standing outside speaking to Dudley, or if he wasn't already outside, he would see me pass from inside the house and come out. so I could see him there. I hated this because my father would always ask me, 'Do you know who I am?' At times I would say no just to piss him off. 'I am yuh fardha.' 'Yay yay,' I would say and carry on walking. No hello or good bye from me. This was embarrassing sometimes if I was with Maureen. One hot summer's day, I was passing 'Teacher's' house, and my father came out and tried to engage me in conversation. He asked me how I was doing at school. I said fine. I decided to ask him if he could buy me

Audreia Josephs

a new pair of glasses. I had hated wearing the NHS free glasses. I was now fourteen years old, and I had been wearing the ugly NHS glasses since I was nine. I had stopped wearing the round pink glasses, but the other versions of the free NHS glasses were equally as ugly. I had tried every colour that they offered, but not one of them improved how I looked or felt in them. Every time I asked my mum about getting a modern pair, she told me that she could not afford them. I was a teenage girl. I always felt ugly in those glasses. My father told me that when I got a job and was working I could buy my own. I thought, 'Really? One day I'm going to show you.' Yet again I felt hurt by his response.

One day I was in my bed fast asleep, when I was awoken suddenly. My mum had come in the bedroom that I shared with Miles and Mary and hit me over the head with her clog. In the 70s, clog shoes were the latest fashion. They were made of a wooden sole and a leather top. These were styled from the Dutch wooden clogs. Now I was startled out of my sleep. Was I dreaming?..........No I was not. I felt a second hit on my head, and the next minute there was blood everywhere. 'What have I done wrong?' I thought, 'for her to beat me out of my sleep?' She shouted that I had not washed up a few items that had been left in the kitchen sink. My older brother Robert had heard the commotion and had come running upstairs in time to see her beating me with the wooden shoe. He pulled her off of me and stood in between us. She said that I was no good and that I would never amount to anything. She

Forgiveness: The Journey to Healing the Heart

always said that to me. My brother was about twenty years old and was living down stairs after Auntie Diane and her family had moved out to a new house. We now occupied the whole house. My mum turned and left me crying with blood running down my face. I got up and washed the blood off of my face, trying to tend to my own wound. This would not be the only time that my brother saved me from my mother and her beatings.

I was not the only person living in this house, yet I was the only one who was beaten on a regular basis. My head hurt so much. I wanted to die. I put my legs through the upstairs window and pushed myself to the edge. I was going to jump. I had had enough of this life and wanted to end it. I was about to jump, when my cousin David from next door walked past my window and said, 'What you doing, Audrey?' 'Nothing,' I said to him and climbed back in. My older sister Jane was just coming home from work and must have seen me hanging out of the window while she was walking home. She never liked me and was always only too happy to report what I did to mum. Some of the things that she told mum were true, and some of the things were made up. After she had seen me with my legs through the window, she told mum. I know that she had known what she was doing. She saw how mum treated me, yet she always enjoyed reporting me. My mum called me and said, 'Why yuh so disobedient? Why you Miss Audrey can't behave yourself?' I knew what was coming next. She had beat me with a wooden clog; now more. My body just gave up after the first

Audreia Josephs

WACK with the electric cord. My tender skin was lighter in complexion than then other children. When she beat me, you could clearly see the red marks. She got me and pinned on the ground with her knee in my throat. She beat me until I passed out. When I came back around, she was still beating me. My brother Robert, for the second time in two days, saved me from my mother. He pulled her off by her waist. I didn't know if he walked in just then or if he had already been in the house. What I do know was he yet again saved my life.

School was always a great distraction from my home life. Whenever I had any money, I would buy my favourite biscuits, caramel cookies or custard creams, Wagon Wheels or Jammie Dodgers. Maureen and I always shared everything. If I was late for school, so was she, and if she was late so was I. We even shared detention. Maureen had beautiful long hair, and she knew how I felt about not having much hair. I was still very upset about the lack of my hair growth. My mum had had enough of my constant moaning about it, she made doctor's appointment. Our doctor was a Polish doctor called Doctor Raybekill on Grove Lane. He checked over my head and announced that I had tight scalp and that my hair would never grow. That was his diagnosis for why my hair was unable to grow. I accepted it. If anyone ever teased or called me picky head or dry head ever again, I was now armed with medical information. My family knew the reason why I had gone to the doctor. My older brother Robert was the first person to ask what the doctor had said. I proudly gave him the medical diagnosis,

Forgiveness: The Journey to Healing the Heart

that the doctor had given me and my mother. 'I have tight scalp,' I said. Robert burst in to laughter and so did the rest of the family. Everyone was rolling over with laughter. I was yet again the source of their entertainment. I was so hurt. I wanted to cry, but I was not going to let them see me cry. 'I hate you all,' I said. 'One day you will all see me.'

I had found out from a friend that a summer school took place during our seven week school holiday. The school was hosted at my old school Grove Lane Juniors, and it was free. You only had to pay for any special trips taken outside of school. Most of the children attended this summer school. Here I had met my friend Janet again, the one who had lived in the Grove Lane house with us. Neither of us realised that we had been childhood friends when we met here; we just connected as friends. She would drop off the pardnor money, a saving club that black people do, to Miss Jones who lived on my road, and then she would come to my house with her little cousin. We would spend ages laughing and joking together, and sometimes I would go off to Handsworth Park with her. It was only years later when I met her mother that we realised that we had been childhood friends. But this summer school was a different kind of school learning. It was hosted by Bennie Brown. Some of our teachers were Gilroy Brown and Marcelle. For the first time in my life, I learned about people like Nanny of the Maroons, Sam Sharp, Martin Luther King, Jr., Malcolm X, Sojourner Truth, Marcus Garvey, Paul Bogle, Rosa Parks. I had never heard of these people before. I found it all amazing. I saw people who looked like me and who had done great things. Why had I never heard about all of these people before? Why did they not teach us about them at school? I never liked school history, but yet here I was enjoying it. This summer school opened up a new world that I never knew existed featuring black history at its finest.

When we returned to school after our seven week holidays, Maureen and I were invited to join the Birmingham School's choir. Singing was our passion; we were so excited to be chosen out of the whole school. Our voices were tested. We were both first sopranos. We could both sing glass-shatteringly high notes. We were taken to a centre with children from other schools, and we were placed in groups according to our vocal ranges - first sopranos, second sopranos, altos, tenors, and basses. We were then told that we would be singing Verdi's Requiem. We were each given the song book and told to practice in our various groups. I opened the song book and faced with words that I had never seen before. Verdi's Requiem was written in Latin, and the book was easily two inches thick. I looked at Maureen, and we both started to laugh. We knew that this was going to be an adventure for us. When we finished practicing with the choir, we continued to practice on our way back home and every other opportunity that we got.

My family did not understand. Whenever they heard me practicing, they all teased me. My brother Robert would say, 'Hear

Forgiveness: The Journey to Healing the Heart

Miss Copra.' He said that I was making noise in the house. They did not understand why a black girl would want to sing classical music. Singing made me feel free, and the only person who understood that, was also sharing this journey with me: Maureen.
The day all the separate parts of the choir came together to practice with the orchestra was one of the most magical days of my young life. We all came together to practice in the Birmingham Town Hall. Hearing the sopranos, altos, tenors and basses sing with the orchestra was pure heaven for me. It touched me in a place deep inside, but what was even more magical was that when Maureen and I sang our part with the sopranos, our voices were so crystal clear and high that the other choir members turned around and just stared at us. We knew that we were good, but we never imagined that our voices were so powerful. But there we were, two black girls from Handsworth singing in a choir with hardly any other black children. We started laughing. We always laughed when we were together.

The day came for the choir to sing in the town hall. I had told my family that they were invited, but no one cared to attend. Maureen and I sang our hearts out. We enjoyed it and felt very proud of ourselves. This would not be the last time that Maureen and I would sing in the town hall. We sang with the school's choir for two years until we left school. We sang on BBC Radio and on BBC TV on Songs of Praise, as well as in various other concert halls.

Miles' and Mary's father always sent their maintenance money

Audreia Josephs

through registered post. One day I was just leaving to go to meet Maureen to walk to school together when the door knocked. It was the postman, and he had a letter that needed to be signed for. So I signed, put the letter on the side table with all the other letters and went off to school. When I got home my mum asked me if I had seen the maintenance money. I told her that I had signed for a letter earlier this morning, thought that it might have been the money and had put it on the side table with the other letters. She said that the letter was not there. She asked everybody in the house if they had seen this letter that I claimed I had signed for. Everyone said no. My mum waited a few more days for the maintenance letter to arrive. As the days passed, she became more and more angry. She started accusing me of stealing the maintenance money. I went and got Maureen to tell my mother that I had not stolen any money. Maureen told her that If I had had any money she would have been the one to know. Maureen tried her very best to help my case, but my mother was having none of it. I was found guilty by the court of mum and sentenced to one of the worst beatings of my life. She held me down and chocked me with one hand. She grabbed anything and everything to beat me with. She beat me for what seemed like hours. In between my cries, pleas and passing out, she kept on beating me. Her knee was firmly on my neck, and I could feel my life draining away. I asked God to take me out of this family. I passed out, and when I came to, she was gone. I tried to stand up. Something was not right. I was unable to stand up straight. It was

Forgiveness: The Journey to Healing the Heart

only about two weeks before the school choir was due to sing on the TV programme Songs of Praise. I was well and truly beaten up. My face was messed up. My lip was busted, my eyes swollen and marks all over my body. I still sang with the schools choir on Song of Praise. When I saw the show on TV, I felt proud and sad all at the same time. I don't remember what my family thought about it; I didn't care. I hated every single one of them. I likened myself to Joseph in the Bible. His brothers had sold him, and one day Joseph was the very one who became the shining light, who saved his family's life. I could relate to this story. I knew that I had and was something different to all of them. I felt that they had all rejected me from being a part of their family. They all treated friends and strangers better than how they treated me. I kept thinking, 'Just watch and see who I become when I grow up.' I only wanted them to love me and treat me as a member of the family. Who would guess that I would one day become Mrs. Joseph in real life? After that beating, I could not stand up for four months. I had no idea what had happened to my left side, all I knew was that I could not stand straight. I got in trouble for not standing up straight in school. No one in my family seemed to notice that I was not walking upright; maybe they just didn't care. The only person who knew about the whole situation was Maureen. She was so very supportive, but she could only do so much at only 15 years old.

    About four weeks after my beating, mum was back up to her old tricks of searching through pockets for evidence of infidelity. This

Audreia Josephs

time she didn't find what she was looking for. Instead she found the letter that had come with the maintenance money. My stepfather John 'Neckep' had taken the money, and had lied to my mother when she had asked if anyone had seen it. He had sat in the bedroom and had heard my screams, pleas and cries, and he had said nothing. He knew that my mum had beaten me badly, and he had said nothing. My mum came and told me that she had found the letter that had come with the money in John's pocket. I said, 'SEE? I told you that I had not taken it, but you didn't believe me. You never believe me. Even Maureen told you. Look at what you did to me? This is the second time that you have taken a man's word over mine.' She gave me a halfhearted, 'Sorry.' It was many years later when I had to have an X-ray for something else that I found out that she had broken my rib, which was the reason why I had been unable to stand up straight. To this day I still experience problems on that side of my body. I decided that I was going to punish my mother and John 'Neckep' for what they had both done to me. One day when the two of them went out for the day, I set my plan in to motion. They kept their bedroom door locked, but I knew how to get in. I made sure that no one was in the house. I used to go in and watch TV when they were not there. Theirs was a token meter TV. You could watch it for about 50p for a few hours, and then you would have to add more money. They used to wonder how come they were always putting money in to the TV. I also found a way of getting the money out of the TV meter. Now for my biggest and brightest idea. I

Forgiveness: The Journey to Healing the Heart

searched through my mother's jewellery box and took what I thought was valuable. I also searched John 'Neckep''s suitcase and found his wedding ring. He had only ever worn the ring on the wedding day, so he didn't need it. 'That will do nicely,' I thought. I took my stash to a very well-known pawn shop in the City Centre and sold the lot. I was sure that the shop owner could see that I was underage, but he bought the items from me anyway. Money in hand, I did not feel one ounce of guilt. I walked all around town having fun with my new money. I also cut up some of my mother's dresses and burnt her afro wig. When they got home and discovered that things had been moved or destroyed, they were mystified as to how this could have happened when the door was clearly locked. I was not sure what John 'Neckep' was looking for when he discovered that his wedding ring was missing, but all I heard was that his ring was missing and that he wanted to know where it had gone. No one asked me anything. Why would they? The door was locked, and whenever it was opened, one or the other was in the room. It was a great mystery, until I grew up and told them that I had stolen it and sold it.

I was changed after all of the years of beatings that I had suffered at the hands of my mother. I didn't care about anything. I became more of a tomboy. I used to skip school and go off with the boys. Everything the boys did, so did I. If they climbed railway lines, so did I. My male school friends said that I was one of the boys. I could fight just like them. Maureen never joined me on these excursions. She was a

Audreia Josephs

serious student. It was now 1976, and I was 15 years old. My older male cousins had a music sound system and used to play out on Murdock Road every weekend. I wanted to go out, but the dance started at about midnight. I decided to sneak out of the house when everybody in the house was fast asleep. I had laid out the clothes that I was going to wear in a bag, hidden in the house. I listened very carefully and made sure that everyone was asleep. I had my own room and no longer shared a room with my younger brother and sister. I put some clothes in my bed, to make it look as if I was still in bed, just in case someone checked. I crept out of my bedroom and climbed down the stairs one at a time. I knew which stairs creaked, so I carefully stepped over those. I got to the bottom of the stairs and went to retrieve my hidden clothes. I got dressed, put my hat on and then wrapped my head with some cloth. My hair was too short for my head wraps to look nice, so I wore hats under my wraps. All of this done under cover of dark. Fully dressed now, I opened the back ground floor window and climbed out. I made sure to close the curtains back. I had a way of hooking and unhooking the window latch to make look as if it was closed. I stepped carefully out of my garden and ran up the road.

Smoking and drinking and partying at 15. My cousins were cool. They kept an eye out for me. I always felt safe around them, and I would always see a few of my friends as well. I was never sure if they knew that I had snuck out of my house. I continued this for a few months. One day I climbed back in to the house at about 6 a.m.

Forgiveness: The Journey to Healing the Heart

on Sunday morning. I could not be bothered with getting changed back into my nightdress downstairs with how cold it was, so I headed straight upstairs. I was busy trying to miss the stairs that creaked when I heard my mother chasing the cat that we had out of her bedroom. Somehow the cat must have snuck into her room and had gone to sleep I stood still, hoping not to get found out.

My mother got to the top of the stairs. When she saw me all dressed up in her best blouse and shoes, she realised that I was just coming in from a night out. 'Weh yuh ah come from?' Where are you coming from? 'Yuh tink sey yuh ah woman.' You think you're a grown up woman. 'Jus ah come in at 6 O clock ina de morning? In my blouse?' I ran past her, before she could think about hitting me. I locked myself in the toilet. 'Robert,' she shouted to my brother, waking the whole household. 'Yuh see yuh sister just ah come ina de house?' Mum was shouting, 'You better get out of that toilet, before I chop this door down with my machete.' I stayed in that toilet for the best part of the day. Robert spoke to me through the door. He asked me where I had been. I told him, 'Out.' He said, 'Mum looks like she's going to kill you, but don't worry about her.' Come out he kept saying. I did not trust anyone, so I stayed where I was. When I did eventually come out from hiding in the toilet, the drama had died down. All she did say to me was that two women cannot live in the same house.

One day I went to school as normal, but when I got home everyone was distressed. It took some time to gather any kind of

Audreia Josephs

information. All of our out-of-town family was here, moving between our house and Uncle Grant's house next door. It was mid-week, so why were they all here? No one had bothered to cook anything. The younger children were just running around. The grown-ups were angry and upset. I could hear Auntie Sweetie crying and screaming from next door. She was also making a strange deep moaning sound. One of the children said that Auntie Cassie had died. I told them that they were lying. I later found out that it was true. Auntie Cassie had been murdered by her partner. The best auntie in the world was dead? I was shocked, confused and numb. I was numb for a long time after that. No one knew how close we were or how much I loved her. She was only 39 years old and died leaving seven children behind.

About a month after we had laid Auntie Casssie to rest, I got home from school and my mum said to me, 'Come with me.' I had no idea where we were going. We went to Lozells. We went in to this building, and we were shown a room. A woman came in, and my mother started saying, 'I want to put her in a home.' I had not been aware that this building was a Social Services centre. She had brought me to this place so that she could get rid of me. I started to cry and asked her why she was doing this to me. 'Yuh too bad, and I've had enough of you.' The woman was telling her that they were unable to take me and that there was a process that she needed to go through. When my mum realised that they were not going to take me, she left. A few weeks after that event, my mum gave me instructions to clean

Forgiveness: The Journey to Healing the Heart

up the kitchen. I cleaned everything that I could possibly clean. I was proud of my effort, but my mum had a way of finding fault with everything I did. Nothing I ever did was good enough. I looked over the kitchen over and over again, just to make sure that I had gotten everything right and to her standard. I had emptied and washed all the Tupperware containers. I dried them, and refilled them all. I thought, 'There is nothing in this kitchen for her to find fault with.' As soon as my mother got home, I said that I had cleaned up the kitchen. She walked in, coat still on and took a look at my handy work. I didn't see her next move coming. She held on to the sweeping broom and swung it like a golf club straight to my head. It made contact, and I was thrown to the other side of the room. I was in shock and started to walk away. The next minute I was on the ground in the hallway. I had collapsed. There was blood everywhere. When I came back around, my younger sisters Jade and Mary started crying when they saw the blood. My older sister rushed to where I was. She was in a panic. And my mother just walked past me as if I was not there. All she said was that I had not dried up one of the Tupperware containers before I had put the peas in it. Jane managed to help me up on my feet. She looked at my head and said that we needed to get to the hospital immediately. She put a towel around my head and held it in place for me. I didn't know what my sister was seeing, but she decided that it was bad enough to get me to the hospital as soon as she could. My mother did not come to the hospital with us. Jane spent all day at the hospital with

Audreia Josephs

me. She had recently cornrowed my very short hair, and now they had to cut out a part of my new cornrow so that they could see they injury. I had a head injury and needed seven stitches in the right side of my head.

    The doctors at the hospital asked how I had gotten this injury. I told them that I had fallen off of a wall. Jane gave me side glances when I said that. When the doctor left, she said that I should have told them the truth so that they could lock up our mum for what she had done to me. For the very first time, I saw compassion in my sister Jane's eyes. She kept saying how wicked and evil mum was. When we got back home, our mum acted as if she had done nothing wrong. I made up my mind that she was never going to beat me or hit me ever again. If she ever hit me, I would fight her. She would have to kill me next time. I might have told the hospital a lie about how I had gotten the injury, but I was not going to lie to everyone else. I told everyone what she had done to me. I told Auntie Sweetie. Auntie asked her why she had done it, and she told Auntie that I had not dried the Tupperware container and that I was bad. No one believed her lies anymore. I told her that I would tell the police about what she had done to me if she ever touched me again, and then I did not speak to her for four weeks. When I needed money for school, I would steal any money that I found around the house. I wasn't going to ask her for anything. I had to go to school with part of my hair missing and stitches in my head. Every time I moved, my head hurt as if she had just hit me again. Now I had

Forgiveness: The Journey to Healing the Heart

a matching pair of head injuries, one from when she beat me with her wooden clogs two years earlier on the left side of my head and now this new injury on the right.

We used to watch Miss World on TV, hoping that one day we would see something special. In 1976, Miss Jamaica made the finals. When Miss Jamaica Cindy Breakspear won Miss World, our house went crazy. We rejoiced and celebrated. We put on music and danced. Up until then, the word Jamaican was usually connected to crime. In the UK if a black man did something bad, it would be announced that he was a Jamaican. It didn't matter what Island or Country you came from - if you were black you were Jamaican. We hated this disrespectful description. Miss Jamaica Cindy Breakspear's victory positively put Jamaica on the map. We went back to school with our heads held high. The British newspapers ran a story about Cindy Breakspear that said she had been dating a Rasta man called Bob Marley.

In the 1970s, many of us British black children started to identify with the Rasta movement. We connected with people like Bob Marley. Many of us started to grow locks. Our parents did not understand. Many of the young people my age were being thrown out of their homes for trying to find their identity. Our parents did not understand that we were facing racism every day in one form or another. Some of the boys in my school started growing locks, and our school tried to ostracise them.

1977 was my final year in secondary school. It was exam time. I

Audreia Josephs

had taken five CSE exams and was now waiting for the results. We had a careers officer come into our school to tell us what options we would have when we left school. Not one of us was encouraged to attend university. Most of us were told to find factory jobs. In 1977 my inner city school did not have high expectations for black children. This was the same year that the mini-series called 'Roots' came out. 'Roots' shocked us. For the first time in our lives we saw what slavery looked like. We became aware of what our ancestors had gone through. When we went back to school all we could talk about was Roots. We became angry. Some of the white children started calling us Kizzy and Kunta Kinte, characters in Roots. That was grounds for a fight.

On our final day at school, we all threw flour and eggs over each other. That was our parting gift for one another. I was now old enough for my mother to allow me out with my friends. Friday night was our Kung Fu night at the Elite Cinema. Most of the young people in the area met up there. It was pure jokes and entrainment, watching Kung Fu movies. The peanut seller man would come in and start shouting, 'Peanuts, peanuts!' Someone would stand up and start doing the same Kung Fu moves that we were watching on the screen. In the same cinema, I saw The Harder They Come. Everybody came dressed in their finest, and Elite was packed to its fullest capacity. Inside the screening was a party. When the film came on, people danced in the aisle. For those of us born in England and who had never been to the Caribbean, it was an opportunity to see the real Jamaica, the one that our families

Forgiveness: The Journey to Healing the Heart

remembered. And for all those who had been born in the Caribbean, well, you could see how homesick they were. I loved it so much that I went to see it three times.

My mother started attending an African church. They all wore white gowns and head dress. It was all so strange. Mum stated inviting these people back to our home so that they could hold services. We were all expected to attend. We started attending these services in London and in various other places in the UK. Mum got baptised and started wearing the white gowns. The elders started pressuring us to get baptised as well. I could not stand the pressure and caved in, saying yes to getting baptised. I was baptised in the afternoon, and in the evening I told my mother that I was going to visit Maureen. I then went off to a young people's party, at Rosehill Road Community Hall. I danced to Burning Spear, Fred Locks, Mighty Diamonds, Big Youth, U Roy,Third World, Asward, Steel Pulse. I enjoyed my evening out, away from the white clothing and incense.

I got my exam results. They were not that good. I was not a great student, so I did not expect any great results. I got B- in Art and in Religious Education and a C in everything else. I wanted to become a fashion designer. I loved art and drawing, so I thought it would be a good combination. I got the bus and went to Bournville College in Selly Oak. They were having an open day. I spoke to the tutors about enrolling in a design course. I was told that I would need to have a CSE sewing qualification to get into the course. In secondary school, I had

Audreia Josephs

spent most of my time being sent out of the class and standing in the hallway, so I knew that this life was not going to be for me. I did not pursue it.

Forgiveness: The Journey to Healing the Heart

CHAPTER 7
Dramatic Changes

In the summer of 1977, there was a heatwave. The pavements started melting, and the gas, water and electric were being cut off. At the time, the unions controlled Britain, and almost everyone seemed to be on strike. During the water strike, each road was given a tank with water in it that was meant to last the whole street for the duration of the strike. We would have to fill empty bottles, pots and pans just to make sure that we had enough water when we were inside. Meanwhile I met a young man called Omar, who professed his undying love for me. Omar was a very tall, light-skinned young man with green eyes. He was captivated by me. I had never kissed him or held his hand. I was still insecure with myself, and I did not believe him when he said he loved me. Omar begged me to go out with him. My family thought it was funny to stand at the window and watch Omar on his bended knees, begging me to be his girl. Around this same time, I got my first full-time job. I had been shown a few job descriptions. I had gone to the Careers Office on Soho Road to find out what kind of jobs were available. I told them that I liked Art. The woman behind the desk said that if I liked Art then I would possibly like this particular job. She

Audreia Josephs

handed me the card and gave me the address to go for an interview. The job was in the jewellery quarter. I went for the interview and got the job at Turner & Simpson. Turner & Simpson was a medal, badge and trophy company, and I was employed as an enameler. I enamelled nurses and school prefect badges. Ironically when I was still at school, I would never have been considered for a prefect position. Now here I was enamelling the badges. I also enamelled silver and gift spoons. While working at this job, I met a young man in the company called Keith. Keith was a soft-spoken, friendly young man. He was one year older than I was. We got on well, and before long we started going for lunch together. I liked Keith, and Keith liked me. We were the only black people in the company. Omar had taken to meeting me every day after work. So now I had to ask Omar to meet me around the corner so that he and Keith would not meet. I kept telling Omar that I did not want to go out with him, but somehow he still had hopes of us being together. Keith asked me out on a date, and I had to tell Omar that I was now with Keith. Omar was heartbroken. I felt bad, but got on with my life. I was still only sixteen.

    Keith and I arranged our first date. Since I was now working, I was able to buy my own clothes. I bought a pair of light blue platform shoes. I went and got my short hair pressed straight with the hot iron comb and then curled it with the curling iron. The lady who did my hair was called Mrs. Barnes. Mrs. Barnes' hairdressing shop was on the corner where Holiday Road met Soho Road. You entered through

Forgiveness: The Journey to Healing the Heart

a door on Holiday Road and walked up to the third floor. Mrs. Barnes was a very skilful hairdresser and had lots of customers. When was my turn, I sat in the chair. She put the iron comb on the gas fire and started to straighten my hair. My hair was so short that while she was working, I thought that the hot comb was going to burn my scalp. I jumped, and she burnt my ear. I let her finish my hair. My hair looked nice. I had never seen it like that before, done up with tiny curls. I was upset with myself because I would have to go out with a burn on my ear. I got back home, had my wash and got dressed in my burgundy maxi dress. My little sister Jade thought it was funny to keep running in and out of my bedroom every two minutes while I got ready. She was now almost five years old, but she was the size of a nine-year-old. I thought that at the rate she was growing, she would be my height by the time she was eight. I was only five foot tall then. I put on some lipstick, and Jade wanted lipstick, too. I sprayed some perfume. Jade wanted me to spray some on her as well. I thought, 'This annoying child. I would love to put a pillow over her face now.' But I smiled at her and sprayed some perfume on her, just to get her out of my room. I put on my new platform shoes, but when I tried to walk in them, I was walking like a baby lamb. I could hardly walk in these shoes. 'I've bought them now, and I'm going to wear them.' I put on the bomber jacket that my mother had brought back from America and hobbled down the stairs. All the family was waiting to take a look. I stood up straight and put one foot in front of the other. Everyone was in the

Audreia Josephs

dining room, except Jane. She had moved out some time ago. My mum said, 'Yuh favour smaddy,' meaning 'You look presentable.' The doorbell rang, and I hobbled on my shoes to open it. There was Keith. He looked really nice out of his work clothes. He smiled. I said hi. When I turned around, my younger brother and sister where standing there with cheeky smiles on their faces. I invited him in, and introduced him to my family. We left and walked up the road towards the bus stop. On the walk to the bus stop, Keith noticed how slowly I was walking and asked me what was wrong. I told him about my new shoes. He linked my arm through his, and we walked slowly together. I looked back towards my family home, and there they were, all standing at the window, watching Keith and me walking up the road. We got the bus to the City Centre. We walked very slowly to the Futurist Cinema on John Bright Street and watched Saturday Night Fever. I loved that movie. All the singing and dancing. After the movie we went to Wimpy for a burger. After that first date, we continued going to the movies together every week.

I had always wanted to learn a language, so now I decided that I would attend night school. I wanted to try to build positivity in my life and invest in myself. I had walked past Handsworth College for the past ten years. I was curious about the inside of the building, so I got a prospectus. I saw that they had a class in learning German in the evenings, so I promptly signed up. On the course, I met and made friends with a girl called Cleaver. She was an immaculate young

Forgiveness: The Journey to Healing the Heart

lady. I loved her style. She did not look or dress like anyone I knew. She told me that she was a window dresser for Ravel's Shoe Shop on Corporation Street in the City Centre. I hadn't even known what a window dresser was before she told me. Meanwhile my friend Valerie Ann, Carmen and I all started learning martial arts together. We found a very good teacher named Ken. We trained at the Methodist church on Wheeler Street. We all loved the discipline. We were very fast learners and got very good at it. It was a time of learning and friendship, despite my life's circumstances.

    Keith and I worked happily with each other. It was soon getting closer to Christmas, and the company would be having a company party. We were both going. In October, I went shopping in the City Centre for a dress to wear to the Christmas party. I found the dress I wanted in a shop called Bus Stop on New Street. The dress was a bright red satin, Chinese style, with slits on both sides. I tried it on, and it was a perfect fit. It looked amazing on my 20 inch waist, and I had a 36 inch chest. The dress cost 25 pounds, and at the time I was only earning eight pounds a week. I also had to give my mum money out of eight pounds. I paid a little bit towards that dress every week, and just before Christmas, I finally got my dress. I also got a new pair of high heel shoes. I set aside time to practice walking in them after that first shoe disaster. I got all dressed up, and we went to the Christmas party. My coworkers had never seen me dressed up and were truly shocked. I loved the, 'Don't you look nice, luv' that they kept saying in their thick Brummie accents. We all ate our Christmas meal. After we had eaten, they had various competition games. I entered the lovely legs competition and won. Miss Lovely Legs, 1977. I won a bottle of wine and some money.

Christmas in our family was a grand affair. It felt like we were nonstop cooking in our home. My mum always made sure that the table was laden with food. Our breakfast started with ackee, saltfish, callaloo, plantain, fried dumpling, both fried and boiled breadfruit, baked ham, bammies, boiled yam and green bananas, fried eggs, baked beans and harddough bread. After we had eaten a heavy load of food, we all feel asleep and were unable to eat our Christmas dinner until about 10pm.

Keith had taken me to meet his family for the first time that Christmas in 1977. They were very nice to me and had bought me Christmas gifts. His brother bought me a lighter. I had met Keith's brother Tom a few weeks earlier at a party. I loved the gift, but when Keith's mother and aunt realised that I smoked, they both seemed to change their attitude towards me. His mother said, 'Young ladies don't smoke. Do you smoke, Audrey?' I felt awkward and wanted to leave. Keith's brother Tom saw how uncomfortable I had become and said to me, 'Don't take any notice of them.'

In the New Year of 1978, our martial arts team was given the opportunity to attend a championship contest in France. It was the first time that I had ever been out of the country. I got my first ever passport. It was so exciting. We took a coach to Dover and then got the ferry to France. I was really sick throughout the ferry journey. When we arrived in France, we discovered that the hotel that had been booked for us in Paris was substandard. We complained, but we were stuck with it. So we made the most of it and made up our minds that we were going to kick some ass in the competition. The smell of baking bread was everywhere we went in Paris. We didn't get a lot of time for sightseeing, but I did love the French clothes that I saw. I loved the smell. It was the first time that I had ever eaten a croissant. And in the end, we did kick ass in our competition.

    I started to get bored working at Turner & Simpson. They kept asking me to make tea for them. I kept thinking that I was not employed to do this. The English drink tea at least ten times a day. I did not mind doing making it once or twice, but when it started taking me away from my job repeatedly, I got pissed off. Plus I did not drink tea. So I started drawing the line. The cups and tea pot looked so stained and disgusting that I got a Brillo pad and scrubbed them out. I felt proud of the gleaming white cups and the shiny teapot, but I was told off by Rose, the supervisor. I was told that I had taken the flavour out of the teapot and cups by scrubbing them. That was all it took. I had had enough of them. I told Keith that I could not stay in this job because I could not see myself moving forward in the company. Keith understood and was very supportive. I found another job at BusyBee Kitchens and Bathrooms. I was employed as a book keeper

Audreia Josephs

where I was trained to put everything into the filing cabinet. I was trained how to enter ledgers in to the book, and I was also taught how to create invoices. This was way before the computer took over the world. Things had to be done manually. I spent a few months in that job before the company was moved from Broad Street. So there I was without a job. My mum kept saying that she wanted me out of her house, and I had had enough of her. I did not have anywhere to move to, but hearing her tell me to go everyday was more than enough.

My older sister Jane had given birth to a lovely baby boy called Andrew and had moved to Magdala Street in Winson Green, not far from my old secondary school. I asked her if I could move in with her, and she said yes. I went home and packed all of my clothes. Miles and Mary were clearly upset at the sight of me moving out and did not want me to leave. Jade on the other hand did not care one way or another. I moved in to Jane's house, but I only spent two days there before she asked me to leave. I was upset, but I also knew that she had her own dramas.

I had kept in touch with Monica after she moved out of my mother's house. She would still come and visit us from time to time, and I would also visit her in her new home. So now I went to visit Monica. Monica had always said that if ever there was a problem, I could come and stay with her. Monica was now living in a two bedroom flat on Rupert Street in Nechells. I told her about my mother and that I had nowhere to live. She said that I could move in with her

Forgiveness: The Journey to Healing the Heart

and her sons. So I did. Living in Monica's house was fun. My friend Cleaver only lived just around the corner on Rocky Lane. Living so close to Cleaver was great. I was able go around to her house. We loved going out clubbing. When we went out, we didn't want to look like anyone else in how we dressed. Cleaver was, and still is, a style icon. I used to say to her that she could wear a garbage bag and still make it look stylish. She is one of the most creative people that I have ever met. I would go around to her house, and we would design and make our own clothing. We hand made all of our club outfits. Our two favourite clubs were Run Runner on Broad Street and Romeo and Juliet's Queensway. When we got in the club and hit the dance floor, everyone else stopped dancing. Dancing was our thing, and we could dance up a storm. Cleaver loved dancing as much as I did. She taught me the art of putting makeup on. She taught me about using the correct colours for our skin tone. Even though there were no specific makeup for people of colour at that time, Cleaver had a keen eye for finding the right colours. My self-confidence grew so much by just being around her. I became aware of my own individual style. I bleached my hair, and it was now auburn. I also used food colouring to colour the sides red and green. My hair style was a semi high top. I had the Grace Jones look in 1978. One of my favourite outfits was a deep pink, button-up, long-sleeved, baggy jumpsuit. Anywhere I went when I wore it, people would stare at me. My family told me that I dressed like a clown. I was upset and told Cleaver what my family had said.

Audreia Josephs

She just laughed and said, 'They are only jealous because they don't look as fabulous as us.' What my family didn't know or understand was that Cleaver and I were ahead of our time. I never ever felt the need to apologise for being me in her presence.

Soon, however, living at Monica's house started to go downhill. She would cook and feed her children, and then she would wash up the evidence before I got in from job hunting. There were many days when I did not eat, and I started looking very thin. I was so thin that one day I was in the City Centre bumped into someone who had known me since I was a young girl who now took one look at me and said, 'What's wrong with you? You look a mess. I don't ever want to see you look like that again.' That day I took a long hard look at myself and knew that it was time for change. Cleaver had been telling me for months that I should find somewhere else to live, and she was trying to move out of her parents' home herself. I didn't have enough money to rent a private place on my own. Cleaver and I had visited a few accommodations with the view of us sharing rent. Some of those properties had had us running away as fast as we could from the mess that they were.

I was already in the City Centre, so I walked over to Waterloo Street where there was a housing association called Copec. I told them that I was homeless and that I needed somewhere to live. They told me that I would have to go to one of their hostels in Mosley. I went to Revels to see Cleaver. I told her what I had done. Cleaver told me

Forgiveness: The Journey to Healing the Heart

that I had done the right thing. I went and met Keith after he finished work. I told him what I had done and that I was going to move in to the hostel. He also understood and supported my decision. I went back to Monica's house and thanked her for her kindness. I moved in to the hostel the same day. The hostel was on Clarence Road in Moseley. I had never been to that part of the City before. It felt more like prison. We each had our own rooms in the hostel, but they were all about the same size as a prison cell. We all shared a bathroom, and there was a TV and dining room. There were rules like you had to be in at a certain time. You could go out at night but only on two nights of the week, and you had to obtain the night key from a member of staff. You could stay out three nights in a row, but if you stayed out over that you were no long considered homeless. No overnight visitors were allowed. You had to eat whatever they prepared. I was not very keen on English food. I had had school dinners, so I knew what kind of food to expect. I had no choice but to eat it.

    I had not seen Mrs. Drysdale for some time, so I went and visited her. I wanted her to know what had been going on. She told me that she had seen my mum, and that my mum had told her that I had left home, and that she didn't know why or where I had gone. I told Mrs. Drysdale that my mum had told her a lie, and I offered her the whole story.

Audreia Josephs

CHAPTER 8
Birth

My relationship with Keith continued to go well. I would go to visit him or meet him after he had finished work. We had been together for nearly one year. He was a respectable young man and never talked about or made a drama about sex. But now, we had decided that the time was right. He invited me to his house. He said that everyone was at work while Keith himself was on holiday from work. So our moment had come. We were into bed together, but all of a sudden we heard the front door open. I jumped up and grabbed my clothes. We both stayed silent while we got dressed. He went downstairs to see who had come into the house. I stayed upstairs in his bedroom. It was his dad. While he was in the kitchen speaking to his father, I snuck out of the house. I called Keith later. He said that his father had known that I was upstairs and had told him not to use his house for sex. I was so embarrassed. I never wanted to face his father ever again. I was only meant to stay in the hostel for a few months before they gave me a flat, but I ended up living there much longer. I missed my period and went for a pregnancy test at Brooks Centre on the corner of Villa and Hampstead

Forgiveness: The Journey to Healing the Heart

Roads. Most girls I knew went there for family planning or pregnancy tests. My test came back positive. My naive mind thought, 'Oh well, at least the housing will have to give you a house now.' I told Keith. As always he was supportive, but he was equally as worried as I was about how we were going to cope with a baby. We decided not to get married but to continue our lives together. I had met some lovely girls in the hostel: Patsy, Maureen Bo, Thelma, Marcia and Marjorie. I had known Marjorie since we were kids in Farm Street Juniors. It had been nice to see a familiar face in the hostel. We had all come to the hostel because of our different circumstances, and we supported each other, banding together as best as we could. Patsy was pregnant and understood the situation. Maureen Bo was a little older than we were, and she was a church girl. She was always speaking about God and the Bible to us. She worried about me, in a big sister kind of way. She would share her food with me. I told the staff at the hostel that I was pregnant. They contacted Copec housing to let them know.

After my initial visit, I had continued to go back to Handsworth to visit Mrs. Drysdale. I told her about all that had taken place in my life and now about the baby. She said that my mum was walking all around Handsworth telling everyone that I had just packed my things and left. Mrs. Drysdale asked me if I had told my mum that I was pregnant. I told her that I had not even seen my mother for months. She told me to go and tell my mum. I walked from Mrs. Drysdale's house on Layton Road, past Park Gate and over to Whitehall Road.

Audreia Josephs

When I got there, my mum was not there. My younger brother Miles had just gotten home from school. Miles and I started talking. He got cheeky during the conversation and tried to do some Kung Fu moves. I was having none of it and slapped and punched him up. Just as I was punching up my brother, my mum came home. She was mad that I had come to her house and punched my brother. She told me to leave her house. I told her that I didn't care if I ever came back to her house, not even when I had my baby. That was how I announced my pregnancy to her. 'Oh,' she said. 'Yuh ah expect baby?' I left. I was sick every single day during my pregnancy. I was put on sickness tablets. Keith had told his brother Tom about the pregnancy, and his brother was concerned about how we would cope with a baby while we were ourselves so young. Tom told Keith to tell their parents. When Keith's family found out about the pregnancy, they were upset. This was not a part of the plan that they had had for their youngest son. He was told that he should get married to me immediately. The only way that we could get married at that time was in the registry office. We had been to a couple of our friends' weddings there, and Keith had always said that they were sausage machines. In one end, out the other, and he had no intention of getting married like that. To be honest, until now I had never heard him stand up to anyone. We decided not to get married then.

    I was sorry for the way I had treated my brother Miles and went back to apologise. We made up. I had also recently reconnected with a

Forgiveness: The Journey to Healing the Heart

friend called Edris. I had known her since I was twelve years old. She was a friend of my own best friend Maureen. Edris and Maureen were friends and attended the same church. My older sister Jane and Edris' older sister Lurline were also best friends, and they had worked at the same place together. Edris had given birth to a baby boy called Mathew and was now living on Factory Road. I started to visit Edris. She was wise beyond her years, deeply spiritually connected. She taught me so much. I learnt how to care for my baby thanks to watching her take care of her own son. She taught me that if you wanted to do something, you could. I used to spend full days at Edris's house, and at times it was too late to go back to the hostel, which was on the other side of town. So I would have to go back to my mum and ask her if I could stay the night. She said yes, and I ended up staying in my old bedroom, spending three nights a week there until my baby was born.

I had told Cleaver that I was having a baby. 'What do you mean you're having a baby?' she had said. She told me that I was too young to be having a baby. Though she remained very supportive of me, she thought that I had gone through so much in my young life and that there was so much more that I could have done with my life. Meanwhile someone must have told my father that I was pregnant because he just turned up, out of the blue one day, to my mother's house. I happened to be there that day. My father had wanted to act the dutiful father. He said to my mother, 'I hear that Audrey is expecting a baby. What are we going to do?' 'What are we going to

Audreia Josephs

do?' She spat at him. 'Can't you see that she has a big belly in front of her? There is nothing that anyone can do. Are you stupid?' Then she laughed in his face. My father was not amused, but he had to take it.

    I was asleep at my mum's house, when I was awoken by a pain in my back. The pain kept coming. I got out of my bed and knocked on my mum's bedroom door. 'I think I'm in labor,' I said. Mum told me to go and have a bath. While I was in the bath, she came in to see how I was. She called the ambulance and came back and scrubbed my back. She made a joke about my back not being scrubbed well since she had stopped washing me as a baby. We both laughed. I called Keith to let him know what was happening. His mother answered the telephone and told me that she would tell Keith. I told my mum that I would be fine, as Keith was going to meet me at the hospital. This was the exact date that I had been given by my doctor as my due date was Good Friday. I had made plans to go to Edris for the day. I was looking forward to our traditional fish and hard o bread, as well as my bun and cheese. I had made the plans, because I was told that the babies normally do not come on their due dates. I had had a feast planned for my Good Friday, but this baby had other plans for me. I was taken from Handsworth to Selly Oak Hospital because that was where I was registered to have the baby. When I got to the hospital Keith was not there. He only lived about a 20 minute car ride away from the hospital. The doctors came around to me and did their usual tests and checks, but Keith still wasn't there. I asked the nurse to call him for me. His

Forgiveness: The Journey to Healing the Heart

number was on my file. The nurse came back and told me that she had spoken to his mother, who said that he was sleeping. Since nothing was happening yet, she wasn't going to wake him. I was in shock. I asked them to bring the telephone to me. I called the number. I told his mother that I was in labor and that I wanted Keith with me now. She said okay. I called her again a few minutes later. I think that I must have gotten on her nerves because she brought him to the hospital.

It was 7:30 in the morning when Keith finally got there. I had been in the hospital for over an hour. I was so happy to see him. Our son was born at 8:12AM, weighing 8 pounds and 4 ounces. We called him Stephen. Keith was so excited to be a father. I was tired after giving birth to my son, and I fell asleep. I had a dark dream, and I was confused. In the dream I saw my other stepfather, Mr. Slick. The dream haunted me. I woke up and went to look at my baby in the nursery. Later in the evening Keith and his family came to see the baby. Keith's brother was excited to meet his nephew. His father was also happy to meet his first grandchild. We had decided to give Stephen's his grandfather's name as his middle name. On the other hand, while Keith's mother was as happy to meet her grandson as the others, she kept a wall up between myself and her. She announced that she was too young to be a grandmother. I guess that she did not want an 18-year-old for a mother to her grandchild, and Keith was still her youngest child. I just looked her in the eye and asked Keith's brother Tom for a cigarette. I had not smoked during my whole pregnancy, not because I hadn't wanted to, but because the smell of smoke made

Audreia Josephs

me feel sick. I went off to the day room with Tom. I left Keith and his parents with the baby. I lit the cigarette. The very first pull I had spun my head, and I threw the rest away. I went back to the ward, but visiting hours were soon over. When Keith and his family left, I lay on my side and watched my baby in the see-through hospital crib. I was amazed and in wonder at this beautiful human being. I just kept watching him breathe.

I spent a few days in the hospital before we left as a family. Keith came to pick Stephen and me up from the hospital. I had finally gotten a flat on Willows Road which we had decorated and furnished together before the baby had come. Keith had used his savings to carpet the flat to make it more homey, but when his mother had found out that he had used his savings, she complained that he had spent the money she had saved for him since he was a little boy. I was also upset to hear that. Because this was Keith's baby as well as mine, and we were trying to make a life together. We walked into our home for the first time as a family. I was frightened. I knew that I was responsible for this little human being in my arms. My heart was beating so loud. We had made sure that everything in the flat was ready before Stephen was born. I had even brought lots of nappies. I tried to settle into our family life, but I had that dream again about Mr. Slick. I kept saying to myself that it was only a dream. I told Keith about the dream but only after I had dreamt the same dream four or five times. I should have been enjoying my baby, but instead I kept obsessing about this dream.

Forgiveness: The Journey to Healing the Heart

CHAPTER 9
Contrast

Stephen was a lovely baby. My mum loved him. I ended up giving him a nickname. I called him Chucho Bean. Don't ask me what it means. I have no idea. When Stephen was first born, I called my mum every day. Stephen gave me and my mum a kind of new bond. He was growing bigger every day, and soon he was eating solid foods and his baby milk. Every meal that we ate, Stephen ate the same. I blended his meals. Before long, he got so fat. Keith was the only one who was working, and we were very short of money. One day I went to the City Centre to buy a few items with the little money that we had. I needed baby milk, but I did not have enough money to buy it. So I put the milk on top of my pushchair and covered it with my coat. When I got outside the store, I was stopped and held by a store detective and pulled back inside. The police came, and I was charged with shoplifting. I had to attend the magistrate court. I pleaded guilty and was given two years' probation for a first offence. My probation officer was called Joy. I had never met a black woman in this position before. Joy was a kind and beautiful person, both inside and out. Even though I had met Joy through an ugly circumstance, she became an inspiration

Audreia Josephs

to me. She showed me that I could be more and dream bigger.

When Stephen was a few months old, I decided that I needed to go to college and that I also needed a job. I wasn't sure how I could do both. I got Stephen into full-time nursery. My friend Edris told me about a job recruitment agency, the Reed Agency on Cannon Street. I went and signed up with them. My first job with Reed was at the canteen in the Royal Mail sorting office. They had a 24-hour kitchen. I cleared and cleaned tables, and I was also on pot and plate wash duty. I decided to get my Chef City & Guild qualification. I attended the College of Food and Arts for two days a week while I still worked for the agency. When I wasn't working for the agency, I would attend day courses.

Keith's mother Doris never took to me. No matter what I did with the baby, she always managed to find fault. Even how I held my baby was a problem. I had a bully mother and now a bully mother-in-law. Doris was a nurse who only had two children. She both owned and drove her own car. I did not know too many women who drove back then. Keith's family lived in an area that other people considered more up-market. I, on the other hand, came from the wrong side of town. I had made the mistake of telling her about my life and how bad it had been, in the hopes that she would warmed to me. Instead all that it did was give her ammunition against me. When she criticised me, she would say, 'You came from nothing, and we brought you into this family.' She would teach me how to cook and sew, expecting me to stand or sit next to her so that I could learn. I had been brought up to never be rude to my elders, so I was never rude or disrespectful.

I had told my friends Cleaver and Edris about Keith's mother. When we christened Stephen, I had made and decorated all of the cakes. I still loved baking and had gotten really good at it. I had also taught myself how to ice and decorate cakes from the books that I gotten out of the library. I had also made the wine. I had started making home brew wine at the age of 15. I learnt to make wine out of necessity. I had started making rich Jamaican fruit cakes, and these cakes needed wine. Every time I asked my mother for money to buy the wine, she would say that she did not have it. So one day when I was in the library, I decided to look up wine making. I had saved up my money and bought the wine making equipment and had begun making my own wine in my bedroom.

I did not ask Keith's family for anything for the christening preparations. Keith, Edris, my mother and I cooked the food. Margret from downstairs made us some coconut tarts. Margret came from Montserrat and made the best coconut tarts that I had ever eaten.

Edris and her partner Joseph became Stephen's godparents, and Mrs. Drysdale became Stephen's godmother. After the ceremony in the church, we held the reception in our little flat. I had made everything look nice, and my family and friends all came. When it came time for the speeches, Doris made a sarcastic comment about not wanting to be a grandmother, which put most of my family up in arms. Everyone who was in attendance could see how much she disliked me. When challenged about her rude comment at the christening, she said that we had taken her speech out of context and that she had been only joking.

    I took Stephen and Keith to meet Mr. Slick, who I considered to be Stephen's real grandfather since he was the one who had actually raised me. We arrived at his house, and I introduced Keith and Stephen. As soon as Mr. Slick held my baby son, I felt sick. Something turned inside of me. I was not sure what I was feeling. Everyone was laughing and smiling with the baby. Mr. Slick was married. His wife seemed to be a nice lady. They gave us food and drinks, but I did not want to eat anything. I just wanted to leave. I felt angry, and I could not understand why. I had to sit there and smile, even while all I wanted to do was leave. I tried to overcome the dark feeling that was trying to take over my mind.

Keith did not enjoy going out or partying. He was happy to stay home. He was a devoted father to Stephen, and he shared the responsibility of our child with me equally. He told me to go out with my girlfriends, and that he would stay home with the baby. I would go out with Edris and Cleaver. I went to Trinity Road in Birchfield where they had a weekend shubbin or blues dance.

CHAPTER 10
Church

When Stephen was about a year old, Keith's brother Tom (who had very long locks) started going to church and asked me to cut his locks. We had always joked about me cutting his locks, and now that he was in the church, I did. Tom could have passed for Bob Marley's brother, and most of my friends liked him. He was a nice person, and we got on really well. Now that he was firmly in the church, he kept talking to Keith and me about his experience and what had brought him to the church. Meanwhile Edris's neighbour Jeannie had a best friend called Maria who had been brought up in the church but had stopped attending. Her father was a pastor, and now that she was going to be getting married, she decided to go back to the church. Edris and I were invited to the wedding, and it turned out that it was at the same church where Tom now went. Maria kept speaking to us to see if we might begin to attend church. Also around the same time, I bumped into a friend who I knew from Grove Lane Junior School named Jennifer Gee. Jennifer had always gone to the church and had always invited me, even as a young girl.

Audreia Josephs

Now here once again she invited me to the same church. It seemed that this church was calling me, so Keith and I decided that we would visit.

On our first visit, we were overwhelmed. There were so many young people in this church, and they all seemed to take an active role. They all smiled and seemed to be having fun. I wanted some of their joy. At the end of the service, they had an altar call, and we were invited to the front of the church. Someone put their hand on my head and started prayed for me. I was asked if I knew that I was a sinner and needed to repent of my sins. I didn't fully understand what was being said to me. All I knew was that I wanted to get rid of this dark feeling. I was asked if I want to wash away my sins in baptism. I said yes. I didn't know where Keith was. When I opened my eyes, the whole church was dancing, clapping and singing. Keith must have said yes as well. The pastor's name was Pastor Woods. He was now announcing to the church that we would be baptised on Tuesday. 'Tuesday,' I thought. 'It's now Sunday.' In two days' time I would be baptised? This was faster moving than my mother's African church. I thought that we would have had to go through some kind of Bible school before they baptised us. Keith and I were told that now we were a part of the church, which meant we could no longer live together. We were told that if we had sex that it would be a sin and we would burn in hell. If we wanted to be together, we had to get married. I thought, 'What have I done to myself?' My life changed so fast, almost overnight.

Forgiveness: The Journey to Healing the Heart

I gave away all of my records. I threw away my jewellery. I got rid of my trousers and party clothes. When I told Cleaver and Edris That I was getting baptised, they both said that it was happening too fast. I had not told my friends about the dark feelings that had come upon me when Stephen was born or that they had stayed with me. I didn't know how to put them in to words, but I wanted to be freed from them. Keith moved out of our little home. Stephen was almost two years old, and he cried when he saw his daddy moving out. Keith moved back in with his parents and came almost every day to see Stephen. Keith and Stephen had never been apart. Meanwhile, every time Keith came to visit us, he had to be chaperoned, and sometimes he came with his brother Tom. I had also invited Cleaver to the church, but when she went, someone told her that she was a sinner and that if she didn't repent she would go to hell. She was so upset that she left crying, and she told me that she would never come back to my church ever again. I started preaching on the streets. I told everyone about their sins, and before long, I started to think that I was better than regular people. If you were not in my church, then I didn't have a lot of time for you. My mother was still in the African church, but I did not agree with their religious philosophy, so her church brethren and I clashed on interpretations of the Bible.

Cleaver had a fiancé who lived in America. He used to live in the UK, but his family had moved to the States in the 1970s. He had never forgotten his first love, and they had kept in constant communication.

Audreia Josephs

He now wanted her with him. So Cleaver moved to America in 1981. I was happy for her; she was starting a new life. We kept in touch by phone and by letter. I rarely saw my best friend Maureen. She was now at college and modelling. My other friend Janet had started a career singing and was now on tour. The only other friend that I saw outside of the church members was Edris, and it was always nice catching up with her. But in general, we were all just moving on with our lives.

One day I was called in to Pastor Woods' office. Keith had asked him for my hand in marriage, and Pastor Woods wanted to know what my answer was. I took one look at our son Stephen and said yes. Keith and I decided on a date. There were so many young people in the church that there was a wedding almost every week, and so we were only given six months to arrange our wedding. Pastor Woods did not encourage long engagements. He thought long engagements led to temptation. I was still busy working and studying. Keith and I had been saving money together before we had joined the church. Our wedding date was set for the 1st of May 1982. I told my mum that I was getting married in six months. She asked me if I was sure what I was doing. I did not have a lot of respect for my mum's opinion regarding my life, and I just told her yes, I knew what I was doing with my life.

Keith's mum was a part time nurse and dress maker. She had made lots of wedding dresses, so it was decided that she would make mine. I had found a picture of a dress that I liked. Because of our

Forgiveness: The Journey to Healing the Heart

church, it had to be a modest dress. Doris looked at the picture and said she would be able to make it. She had seen some lace and would buy it for my wedding dress. A week later when she showed me the lace, I was upset. I had seen the same sort of lace in the front window of my church sister's houses. The sister had used it for net curtains. Now I felt that my wedding dress was going to be made from net curtains. Doris had made my wedding dress, but I was silently unhappy about it.

Someone - and I can only assume that it was my father's friend Dudley - had told my father that I was getting married. My father sent a message to my mum that he wanted us all to meet. So the meeting was arranged, and we all met at my mum's house. My father was not happy that he had only heard that his daughter was getting married and that he was not involved in the wedding himself. My father wanted invitations for himself and his friends. I gave his family an invitation, but he was upset when the invitation had his partner's, my brother Howard's and his names on it. He said that I had insulted him by inviting him as just a guest. I told him that he had not put a penny in to this wedding so did not deserve to invite any of his friends. My father ripped up and threw the wedding invitation away, and left the UK two weeks before my wedding. I had not asked my father to walk me down the aisle. I felt that if I did that it would be fake, because we had never had that kind of relationship. I didn't invite my stand-in-father Uncle Grant after the way he had treated us. I asked my older

Audreia Josephs

brother Robert to walk me down the aisle. He had been there for me when I needed him. I didn't real care what or how my father felt. He had shown me that he was only interested in showing off to his friends.

    The day of the wedding came. It was a wet, windy and rainy day. I got dressed at mum's house. I had three women help me to get dressed, all claiming to be my mother. One was my godmother Miss Ruby. The other was Mrs. Drysdale. The last one was a friend that I had met just before I had started going to church. Her name was Pee, and she had been my hair dresser. I felt the love from all three of these women. Of course Mrs. Drysdale had taken centre stage in my life. I put my dress on, but it was too short and did not look like the picture that I had given Doris. I could not hot comb my hair - Church rules - so my short hair just looked like short hair. No makeup allowed either, just a plain face. I looked at myself in the mirror and thought, 'This was not how I thought I would look on my wedding day.' I felt sad and did not want to go through with it. I looked like a twelve-year-old girl. I had six bridesmaids, two flower girls and two page boys. My sisters Mary and Jade were two of my six bridesmaids. Jade was ten years old at the time. She was originally going to be a flower girl, but she was as tall if not taller than I was, so we decided to make her a bridesmaid. We bought her high heel shoes to match up with the other bridesmaids, all in their peach dresses. Jade can be seen standing awkwardly in every wedding picture.

Forgiveness: The Journey to Healing the Heart

I was one hour late for my own wedding. I had asked my cousin Maurice if he would drive me to the wedding. Maurice was my mother's cousin and had a Jaguar. But my auntie and cousins had not sorted out cars for themselves, so they all jumped in to my wedding car. Maurice must have made five trips to the church with various family members. Finally everybody was at the church, and it was finally my turn. When we arrived, I started to shake. Robert asked me if I was alright and said not to worry. With my big mouth, everyone thought that I was bold. Little did they know that I was a really shy person. No one would have believed that. My bold personality was a cover for shyness. The church door opened, and everyone turned to look at me, and I shook even more. Robert had to hold me steady all the way up to the front. People were surprised to see how shy I really was.

When we got to the vows in the ceremony - for richer, for poorer - I found myself saying for richer for richer. Everyone in the church laughed. I had not meant to say that; I was just so nervous that the words came out wrong. Pastor Woods made sure I repeated them in the correct order the second time. After the wedding ceremony, we headed to Broadway School for our reception. It was still raining, so we were unable to take any outside pictures. My mum had left the African church and was now attending Austin Road church. The ladies from that church had beautifully decorated my reception hall. Our master of ceremonies was funny and humorous throughout the reception, and afterward we all left. Keith and I were now in the church so we did not lay on a party for our family. It was also our church anniversary, and we would be having an evening service. My family being the party people that they are, had decided to have a party anyway without us. Keith and I went home, changed out of our wedding clothes and went to the anniversary service.

My 21st birthday was the month after our wedding, but no one remembered or celebrated. I told a church sister named Joan, and she baked me a cake week after my birthday. I was grateful. My mum and my younger siblings were all going to Jamaica for the first time. I was jealous. I had wanted to go to Jamaica for a very long time. My mum said to me that my money for a ticket had gone in to a wedding. I couldn't say anything to that.

I had left my wedding gifts at my mother's house, one of which had been a house plant. While my mother was in Jamaica, a family member went into the house and stole the plant and some of my gifts. We had no way of knowing who had stolen them, but I had an idea of who would do something so low down.

After the wedding, I hardly saw any of my family. Pastor Woods placed me in the young people's choir. I attended church on a Monday for tarry service, Tuesday for normal service, Wednesday for choir practice, Thursday for normal service again, Friday for Bible school, Saturday for another choir practice, and Sunday for Sunday service. There was no time for anything else. I started noticing a class structure in the church, and I was definitely on the bottom rung. I started seeing things that I did not like. For example, Keith and I did not have a car,

Forgiveness: The Journey to Healing the Heart

so sometimes we had to run out of church to get our bus home. If we missed the last bus, we would have to walk home, which we had done on a few occasions. However, now I was pregnant with our second child, and we didn't want to miss the last bus home. One night we got up to leave, and Pastor Woods called us out. It was 10 o'clock at night, and he had been speaking for at least two hours, saying all sorts of stuff that was not meaningful. Our last bus left at 10:45PM, and I had had enough of some of the members getting in their cars and driving right past us. This was not how I thought church people behaved to one another. I pushed past the usher so that I could leave.

Audreia Josephs

CHAPTER 11
Curve Ball

There were so many young, married couples in the church, and Pastor Woods had to have a married meeting with us all. We were told when we had our babies that we could use condoms - the boot, as he called it - for six months only and no other form of contraceptive. We were left to the elements of having lots of children but with no real support. I was expecting my second child and was having a hard pregnancy. I was admitted into hospital with an infection. I was fed up. One day Keith's mother came to the hospital to visit me. She only worked ten minutes up the road at the Queen Elizabeth hospital. I told her that I had had enough of being in the hospital. What they were doing for me could have been done at home. She said 'Do you want to leave?' I said yes. So she helped me pack my items, and we just walked out. I left in my nightwear. We did not say a word to anyone. We walked over the grass to her car. Escaping from the hospital was the only fun that I had ever had with my mother-in-law.

About a week later on the 25th January 1983, Nathan was born, weighing 6 pounds and four ounces. He was born three weeks early.

Forgiveness: The Journey to Healing the Heart

Nathan was such a quiet baby. No one could believe how quiet he was. Everywhere I went, people seemed to be fascinated by him. They kept asking what her name was. People thought that he was a girl, even when he had blue on. At first Stephen had said that he didn't like him, but as time went on, he loved his baby brother. Stephen was such a helpful child. He would fetch and carry any thing for Nathan. He even wanted to feed the baby.

Around the same time that Nathan was born, two lovely ladies started coming to church who, I found out, lived only a five minute walk away from our flat. They were two wonderful women called Kim and Grace. They were both older than I was, and they always made me feel like I was their younger sister. They were best friends who shared most things together. Kim had a daughter called Kate, who was six years old. Kim and Grace had come to our flat and had seen how small it was, and they decided that we should come to their house to eat. They all loved my children so much. They loved spending time with baby Nathan, and so after discussing it with Keith, I decided that they would become Nathan's godmothers.

I was still attending college and working on my qualifications in English and Maths. I also learnt word-processing. I even obtained a diploma in caring for the elderly. Meanwhile I still worked for the agency. I was sent all around the West Midlands area as a now qualified chef. I used to turn up at my agency with my chef whites, and the highest bidder could have me. When I first started with the agency,

Audreia Josephs

they use to send me to Central Televisions to clear and clean the tables and wash the plates and pots. When I qualified as a chef, the agency sent me again to work at Central Televisions. The supervisor there was used to me coming to clear tables, so when I got there, I was sent to the pot washing area. I told her that I was now a chef. It felt so good to see the look on her face. She wanted to boss me around, like she used to do. Now when I had finished my job, I stood with the other chefs with my arms folded. It felt good to be in such high demand. I still worked in the Royal Mail canteen, but I was no longer on clearing tables or plate and pot wash. I was either their breakfast chef or their pastry chef.

    Our home on Willows Road was soon no longer suitable. Copec housing had done some work on the roof of the house, and the rain had started getting in. Mould was growing in our bedroom, and we were all sleeping in the lounge. We did not have any space with two young children. I decided that we needed to buy a house. I started getting the weekly newspaper so that I could look at possible homes for us. Keith always left me to take the lead in situations like these. I realised that we would be unable to obtain a mortgage if I didn't have a permanent, full-time job. A brother in the church called Camron had started an interior design company, and he needed a receptionist. I had known Camron before we had gone to church; he was Keith's brother Tom's longtime friend. Camron was also engaged to Joan, the sister who had made me my only 21st birthday cake.

Forgiveness: The Journey to Healing the Heart

I told Camron that I needed a permanent job, and I was given the job of receptionist. Meanwhile I continued to look for a home for us. I saw one in the newspaper, in Erdington. We made an appointment the view the property. It was a three bedroom house, and Keith and I loved it. The owners were very friendly. The house looked beautiful. A few days later, we went to the mortgage broker to find out if we could get a mortgage for this property, and a few weeks after, we were approved and put an offer on the house. The offer was accepted, and we became homeowners. We planned our move-in date. The previous owners had moved out, so we hurriedly went to pick up the keys to our new home. I put the keys in the door, and we walked in. Every room that we walked in to was a complete mess. The rooms smelt of cats and dogs. Windows were broken. When we checked the floorboards, they were full of woodworm. I started to cry. How had I not seen this mess when we had made previous visits? The house had looked great when we had seen it with furniture. We had been tricked, and there was nothing that we could do about it. We now owned the house. We were unable to move in straight away. We had no choice but to stay in our mouldy flat. We had to find someone who could get rid of the woodworm, and in order to do that we had to find extra money that we really did not have to make house liveable. Keith left all of this to me. I had to check out every tradesman and try to get the best price. I managed to get all the tradesmen found and all the work done, but it was three months before we were fully able to move in our new home. One of our church sisters named Jill lived up the road from our new house. She and her family loved my children. Jill and her husband Mike knew that we were repairing our home and offered to keep Nathan for us. Jill had Nathan for a few days. One day at church she told me that when she had taken Nathan out, and someone had asked what his name was but she had forgotten to ask me what the baby's name was. She was embarrassed and worried that someone might think that she had stolen the baby. It was and still is a funny story that Jill and her family still share.

Keith and I began arguing every day between the pressure of going to church every day and his mother's insults. For years Keith, the children and I traveled by bus every Tuesday and most Sundays to visit his family. Doris still put me down and disrespected me in front of her family and my children. Keith's brother Tom was always supportive of me whenever she did that, but Keith would just sit and never say anything to defend me. I was beginning to lose respect for Keith I would ask him how could he continually let his mother treat me like that. He would say, 'What do you want me to do? I'm not going to argue with my mother,' or 'I can't kill her for you. He let her insult me for seven years, and all of it had worn me down. I planned on leaving him. I confided in his brother about how I was feeling. Tom pleaded with me not to leave, saying he would speak to Keith.

I still had the dark feeling, but now the pictures were much clearer. I now knew that I had been abused by Mr. Slick. I felt angry and confused. I didn't know who I could trust or tell. I felt ashamed

Forgiveness: The Journey to Healing the Heart

and unclean.

I learned that I was expecting our third child. I was in shock because Nathan was only one year old. The interior design company that I had worked for had closed down, and I was now working as a receptionist at the Birmingham County Court. I had gotten the job through the agency. There was a vacancy for a permanent position, but I was not offered a permanent job because they found out that I was pregnant and kept me on just as agency staff. I lost one stone in weight during the whole pregnancy. My face and body was so thin. The doctor and hospital staff were worried when I lost the most of my weight during the Christmas holidays. I had almost stopped eating any kind of food. I survived on cake and biscuits. The doctor sent me for a scan to see how the baby was developing, and it showed the baby was developing well. They told me that the baby might be small. I developed a skin rash that covered half of my body. The doctors did not know what it was or how to treat it.

I had just gotten home from my doctor's appointment, and my friend and sister in the church Pat had just come to visit me. Suddenly I felt a sharp pain in my back. I recognised that pain and told Pat that I was in labor. She laughed and thought that I was joking. The pain kept of coming more and more powerfully. When Pat looked at my face, she knew that I was being serious. Pat shouted for Keith, and he came running down the stairs. I told him to get the children's clothes together so he could take them to his parent's home. We now had a car. Tom had bought a new car and had given us his old car. Pat called

Audreia Josephs

the ambulance. The ambulance took some time to get to my house, and when it came, I told Pat that I would go to the hospital by myself. When I got to the hospital, Keith was already there. It was 7 o'clock in the evening. I was taken to the labor ward, and Master Peter was born at 7:10PM. He was born in 10 minutes on Thursday, the 14th of March 1985. He weighed a healthy seven pounds and four ounces. I thought that Keith would be disappointed to have a third son, but he was so excited that he was practically jumping up and down with joy. The rash that had covered half of my body disappeared within a week of giving birth to Peter.

Peter was a happy baby. He had a healthy appetite. In 1985 I was 23 years old, a mother of three young sons and a struggling homeowner. Meanwhile the strangest thing occurred whenever I went to visit my mother with the children. John 'Neckep' always grabbed the children and played with them and gave them money and other treats. He loved my children, and they seemed to enjoy his company as well. This came as a great surprise to me.

    I now had three boys that I had to dress for church every week, but I could not afford to buy new clothes for them every week. I had found a place in Smetwick called BlueGate Market that sold cuts of suit material. I decided to learn how to sew and to start making my children's clothes. I brought a sewing machine from a catalogue. I asked a church sister called Yvonne, who also lived two roads away from me, to come to my house and teach me how to sew. Yvonne was kind and patient with me. I also had another sister from the church

Forgiveness: The Journey to Healing the Heart

who lived nearby called Candy. Between Yvonne and Candy, I learnt how to sew. I learnt more being around these two beautiful young women than I had ever learned sitting next to Keith's mother. Before long I was making little trousers and waistcoats for my sons. My sons were very well dressed. I was so happy and excited by my newfound talent. I happily showed my mother-in-law the latest creation that I made for the boys. She would look the garments up and down, declaring that my work was alright but that the finishing was not good. Whatever I showed her, I always got the same dry reply.

One day some of our church members from America came to the UK. They looked amazing. Their hair was nicely done, and, shock of shocks, they even had their nails done. Now in our church that was a big NO NO! But here were the members of our sister church looking completely different to us. We all looked and dressed like a bunch of old people. Since I had joined the church, I had been criticised by friends and family about my state of dress. I had taken to wearing a beret fully pulled down around my forehead and ears. I wore a coat that would have more suited my mother. I looked 46 when I was only 23. I thought that to look like a Christian, I had to look down-trodden. I had noticed that a few of the sisters who were considered on the top rung of the church social ladder used to relax their hair. I could recognise relaxed hair, though some people couldn't see it. These sisters would walk around with their lovely, long, straight hair as if they had been born with good hair. Here's that stupid term again: good hair. No one dared to say anything to them about relaxing their hair or whether or not it was natural. More and more I could see a disparity in the church.

I had been a very creative style of person before I had gone in to the church. I wanted to feel my style again. I was in the choir wearing a black and white skirt, white blouse and black and white stripped hat every week. Being in the choir was great because I did not have to find clothes to wear to church each week. But when I was not in the choir uniform, I wanted to feel and look like me. I started making clothes that I felt comfortable in. One day I wore one of my creations to church. I was told by one of the older sisters, 'We don't dress like that in this church.' I was modestly dressed. I didn't have any part of me exposed. These people felt that it was their job to tell you how to look and dress.

Two new sisters joined the church, and I loved how they expressed their own dress style and creativity. They would sit in their unusual garments at the very front of the church. I saw the way they were frowned upon. They were non-conformists. They were not taken seriously. Some of the members tried to imply that the two sisters were a bit mad. All of this was just because they chose not to be clones. I kept observing more and more distasteful things about the people in the church.

Pastor Woods was not a natural preacher. His sermons did not flow easily. I had invited my mother to a few services, and she always said that his sermons made her fall asleep. His sermons were usually based around putting someone down without ever mentioning their

Forgiveness: The Journey to Healing the Heart

names. His whole ministry was based on instilling fear. He never spoke about self-empowerment or self-love. A lot of the people in Pastor Woods' church were very much like him. They were self-absorbed, judgmental and lacking compassion. The longer I stayed in that church, the more I became like them. One day the church announced that there would be a convention in Germany. We were told that if anyone was interested that they could put their names down to go to the convention. I had never been on a plane before. It was a three day trip. I put my name down, and I paid the deposit. I decided to leave Stephen and Nathan with my mother and Peter with Frank's family. We would be staying on a US military base. The day came to leave for Germany, and we all met at Birmingham Airport. I was so excited to finally be getting on an airplane. I loved the airplane journey. It was November 1985, and Germany had the coldest weather that I had ever felt in my life. The convention was great. The congregation was fun and light-hearted; they were not as stuffy as the people from my church. The main preacher was Noel Jones, who was the brother of the actress Grace Jones. I had met Noel previously on a few occasions. He was a part of our sister church in America. That brother could preach.

Audreia Josephs

CHAPTER 12
Disappearance

My father disappeared off to America, and Howard and I were corresponding. He was now studying at Birmingham University for his PhD. He came over to our house on the weekends. The boys loved getting to know their uncle. My father had also been in touch with me and would call me from time to time. One day my father called to say that he was coming back to England for a holiday and would like to see me and my family. I still had bitter feelings towards my father, but I said yes. When he arrived in the UK, he called to let me know which day he was going to visit. He said that he would also bring guests with him. I knew that he would come with my brother Howard but could not think who the other guest could be. I had gone shopping in the morning and came back to the house to cook a large spread. The doorbell rang. I saw Howard first, then my father. A young man and young lady stood behind my father. My father greeted me, stepped to the side and said, 'This is your brother and sister. Hug them.' ...... 'WHAT?' I thought. 'WHO?' I invited them in. I told my father that I was too old to only just be learning about another brother and sister. 'Where have you been hiding them?' I said to my father

Forgiveness: The Journey to Healing the Heart

'They live in Bilston,' he said. 'Bilston, England?' I said. 'Only about one hour's bus journey away?' I said. I felt myself getting angry. They were both so lovely. I saw that they felt as awkward as I did. My father sat there smiling. I just wanted to slap him. 'Why have you never told me about them?' I shot at my father. 'I was worried about how you would feel,' he said. 'Lies,' I thought. 'He has never thought about how I felt about anything before.' I turned my head away from him and started speaking to these young people. 'What are your names I asked?' Mavis and Mark, I was told. My sister Mavis was petite and had the same beautiful hazel-coloured eyes as our father. I asked her how old she was. She told me that she was 19 years old. My brother Mark was also a very handsome young man. He had gotten my father's height. He was 17 years old. Howard seemed to know them. Howard's mother was not Mavis' and Mark's mother, so who was their mother? I wouldn't know who she was anyway. I asked them if they had heard about me and their other brother and sisters. They said no. I found out that Mavis was the only girl among three brothers and that she had always wanted a sister. I said to her, 'If you only knew how many sisters you really had.' Mavis was in the church, so we had something in common. Yet again my father had disappointed me. For me his crime was keeping us from each other, not letting us get to know each other earlier. My boys loved them, and they in turn loved the boys. Now that my father had gotten this news off his chest, he went back to America. My siblings and I had now made a connection, and we spoke on the phone regularly. Mavis even had Peter at her house for weekends

Audreia Josephs

These days I was unable to sleep, and my body kept shaking. I went to the doctor, and was given a letter to see a psychologist. However I did not attend the appointment. A voice inside of me told me not to go because I would be alright.

In 1986 I decided that I wanted to meet my eldest sister Gen. She had left Jamaica and was now living in Canada. We had spoken on the telephone but had never met face to face. I worked day and night saving up for a trip to Canada. The day before I flew, I met my mum in the City Centre. She had gone to the bank and gave me some spending money for my trip. I was very surprised but grateful. We went and bought some last minutes items together. I looked in my bag for the money that my mum had given me, but it was missing. Someone had picked my money out of my bag. We were both very upset.

The next day I got a taxi to Birmingham Airport. I was nervous and excited all at the same time. I had never taken a long-haul flight before; this was only my second time ever going on a plane. I had chosen to fly with an airline called Wardair. Every passenger was treated like first class. We were all served on bone china plates, and the whole flight was amazing. I had never seen my sister face-to-face before, and when I landed I was worried about recognising her. We had only ever seen pictures of each other. When I got to Montreal Dorval Airport, I retrieved my luggage and walked out, looking around for a face that looked like mine. There she was, my big sister. We ran and hugged each other. I kept looking at her. We really did look alike. We drove to her apartment where I met my two nephews Wrayon

Forgiveness: The Journey to Healing the Heart

and Teddy and my niece Naomi. It was so good meeting and getting to know my family. We stayed up late in to the night talking about everything. The next day I met another older sister called Carlene, but I did not get a warm reception from her. She was not my mother's daughter. Carlene had grown up in Jamaica with Gen. Carlene did not like me and out rightly told me so. She didn't want anybody to get in between her and Gen. Here I was, British-born and a face like Gen's, and Carlene could not stand it.

    My sister Gen was not a church-going person. She asked me if I went to parties, and I said no. She said you don't have to drink or dance. I told her that if I went to a party with her that I would also take my Bible with me. She laughed. I guess that no one had ever said that to her before. Before I had left the UK, I had been given the address of Pastor Woods' brother's church in Canada. I asked my sister how to find the church, so the next day Gen took me on the bus and showed me how to use the Metro. I found the church and attended for the duration of my trip. They were a kind and friendly group of people. They all took to me, and I made some really good friends. My two weeks in Canada flew by very quickly, and before I knew it, it was time to go back to the UK.

    I had gone back to the college of Food, Art & Design to refine my cake decorating skills. I did confectionery and cake art design City & Guilds. Most of the women on this course were much older than I was. Though I was the baby of the group, I met some of the most amazing

Audreia Josephs

women on this course. These ladies were very supportive of me. They helped me with my coursework when I couldn't think straight. Mrs. Brady, Winnie and Dora. These women supported me during a dark time in my life. There would be a time later in my life when Dora's path would cross mine again.

In 1987 Keith lost his job. He would not get up in time to get to work, so they sacked him. This became a great source of pressure for me. I still worked for the agency, and I also worked nights in an elderly care home. I was finding it hard to keep up with the household bills. Debt collectors started knocking. The very first time this happened, Keith had opened the door. He called me to deal with it. When he left it to me, I knew that our marriage was over. I kept thinking, 'Why can't he be a man?' A few months later, British Gas turned our supply off when we couldn't pay the bill. We were without gas for seven months. For seven months, I prepared our family meals on a one ring electric cooker. At times I had to let our children either stay with my mother or Keith's family.

Every time I left my children with Keith's mother, she always had something negative to say about the state of children's clothes or their health. I could never do anything right in her eyes, and she always had to point that out to me.

Tom announced that he was getting married. 'About time, too,' I jokingly said to him. Tom was marrying a very nice church sister named Rosemary. We sang in the young people's choir together. I

Forgiveness: The Journey to Healing the Heart

started making the boys suits for the wedding. I also started making a dress for myself. As the wedding approached, Rosemary asked me if I would decorate the wedding cake. I designed an amazing, show-stopping cake, while someone else baked it. I worked on the decorations on this cake and was truly happy with the outcome. On the day of Tom's and Rosemary's wedding, Doris was meant to bring a tablecloth for the wedding cake table. I waited for hours for Doris to come with the cloth, but in the end I decorated the table as best as I could. It was a complicated cake design, but I was so proud of it. Keith had made a special stand for the cake. Tom had always been the best brother-in-law and uncle to my children that anyone could have wished for, and I wanted to make sure that he and Rosemary had the best. After decorating and setting up the cake, I got home with only an hour to spare for getting ready. Keith had already dressed the children, so I quickly got myself dressed. We got to the church just in time. Halfway through the service, Keith's mother turned up. I was shocked. In my opinion, Tom was her favourite son. But as soon as she sat down, she started elbowing her husband in the ribs. I'm still not sure what that was about. It was even captured on the wedding video. When the service was over, I headed to the reception hall to check on the cake. I was in shock when I saw it. Someone had moved it, and it was tilted on one side. It was sitting on this mystery table cloth that should have been there hours ago. Now I saw the reason why Doris was late for her favourite son's wedding. She had obviously got to the reception hall after I had left, moved the cake to put the table cloth on and had no idea how to put it back up. I was so happy that I had gotten to the hall before the bride and groom did. I quickly put the cake in order.

Tom had gotten married on his birthday. When it was time for his mother to give her speech, she said, 'Rosemary welcome to the family.' Rosemary was Doris's dream daughter-in-law. 'Call me mom.' Wow. She had never said that to me in almost ten years of knowing me. Then Doris took the couple into the centre of the hall where there was something covered up with a cloth. Doris and her sister Milly unveiled a four-tier cake with all the ceremony that they could muster. She said that this was Tom's birthday cake. I sat there thinking, 'It looks more like a wedding cake.' Every time I tried to speak to Doris at the wedding reception, she made me feel dismissed, waving her hand as if she was swatting away a fly. I knew my place in that family.

After Tom's and Rosemary's wedding, I felt hurt at how Doris had made me feel. I told Keith that I was not going back to his parents' home. I only felt bad about Keith's father. He loved his grandchildren. Nathan had spent a few weeks with his grandfather when I was carrying Peter. My children's grandfather had been made redundant the year before. He was used to working and was now at a loss for what to do. He had redecorated his whole house and was now bored. 'Gimme mi da bwoy dehe,' he would say. He and Nathan became partners in crime. Every time I saw Nathan, he was eating. He got so fat spending time with his granddad. In January we found out he was unwell, so I took the day off and went to visit him. I went during the day because I did not want to see Doris. During my visit, he kept saying, 'If massa God

Forgiveness: The Journey to Healing the Heart

want to...' and I kept cutting him off mid-sentence. I didn't want him to do the death talk. He got worse and was taken to the hospital. On the 25th of January 1988, my children's grandfather passed away. He passed away on his grandson's 5th birthday. There were no birthday celebrations for Nathan that day. Even though I had had my children at a young age, I was really glad that their grandfather had gotten to know his three grandsons. He knew that his name would live on through them.

Doris made me feel uncomfortable even during the funeral preparations. I offered to help her out in any way possible, but she hardly spoke to me. A week after the funeral, Tom, Rosemary, Keith, myself and the children were all at Doris's house. After we had all eaten, I went upstairs to make a call to a friend on the house phone. I always used to pay for any calls that I had made. I was in Keith's old bedroom on the phone, when all of a sudden the door was thrown open. 'Get off the phone,' she shouted. 'The phone is only for family. You are not family!' I looked up at her and said, 'What?' Doris said again, 'Get off that phone.' I told the person on the other end that I had to go. 'You are not family,' she said to me. 'My husband died of a broken heart because of you,' she shouted out at me. 'What do you mean?' I could feel the tears ready to erupt. 'He died because you stop bringing the children to see him.' Tom heard the commotion and came upstairs. He asked me what was wrong and why I was crying. I told him what his mother was saying to me while she stood there. He told his mother to go and have a rest in her room. He said 'Don't take any notice of mum. She's just upset. And you know that dad did not die from a broken heart. You know it was a disease that took him.' I was grateful for Tom's kind words, but I just wanted to get out of that house with my children. I had to wait while Keith sat there with smiles and comforting words for his mother.

After his father's death, Keith became completely unresponsive. He would not even try to find a job. I had spoken to a few people who I had trusted about the situation. People knew that Keith was not working and needed a job, and they brought application forms from their offices or other jobs for him. The application forms sat unfilled around the house for months. I felt embarrassed that people had gone out of their way to try to help us and Keith had not responded. He behaved and looked normal whenever we went to church. So I also tried to make the world think that we were just a normal family.

I was still not sleeping. Every time I went to a doctor to find out what was wrong with me, they always tried to get me to see a psychologist. Something deep down inside of me kept telling me not to go. I was also still working two jobs and attending college.

Nathan started reading at the age of three. He was a very advanced reader. When he started going to school, the school called me in to say that Nathan would not communicate. I didn't understand. He was a very quiet child, but he was always reading to us at home. They wanted the school psychologist to come in to see him. I was not going to let them do that to Nathan. I kept telling the school that there was nothing wrong with Nathan. This went on for eighteen months.

Forgiveness: The Journey to Healing the Heart

After fighting with the school for so long while trying to cope with everything else in my life, I ran out of energy and gave up the fight. I ended up sending my son to an independent school out of town.

I felt constant hate and resentment towards Keith. We argued all the time. I kept thinking about how I could leave Keith. Where would I go? Where would I live? The opportunity came to get away and have a break. I booked a heavily discounted flight to Canada and stayed with some friends from the church in Toronto. I had left the UK so quickly that I had not even told my sister that I was coming to Canada. I called Gen and told her that I was in Canada. 'You're where?' she said. I told her that I would be going to America from Toronto. My older brother James (Jim) had been living in America for some time now, and he was not very far from where my father lived in New York. The brethren in Toronto was going to New Jersey for a conference. I went to the US Embassy and obtained a visa to travel from Canada to the States. We traveled by minibus. I was excited, because I had never met my brother face-to-face before. I had told him where we would be, and when he pulled up, I shouted, 'There's my brother!' Everyone laughed at my British accent.

My brother was a cab driver, so he knew most of the places around town. He stared at me. 'Yuh look like mum,' he said. He was a giant, standing at seven feet and two inches. I'm not even sure if I had ever met anyone that tall before, and here he was, my brother. I thought, 'What happened to me? How come I'm so short? Jim got all the height! At least I'm taller than my mum.' I stayed at his apartment

Audreia Josephs

in Brooklyn, and I cooked him a few meals there. He was surprised that his British sister could not only cook but could do it well. I had so much fun with him. He would drive me all around New York, keeping me in the car while he worked and would tell the passengers that I was just being dropped off later than they were. The passengers were all fine with my presence, especially when they heard my British accent. Jim was just as big of a kid as I was. He made me think what it could have been like if he had grown up in England with me. He would not have left me out the way the others had. We went to visit our father together. My brother Jim had a different relationship with our father than I did. I was more distant to my father. I could not summon up any kind of energy to pretend that I was excited to see our father. When we got to Dad's house, I could see that Jim wanted me to interact more with our father, but I found it hard to interact and converse with a stranger. That's how I saw my father; he was a stranger. I sat down and started watching whatever was on his TV at the time. I felt put on the spot every time Jim tried to get me to join the conversation. We really didn't have a conversation outside of how are the children, husband and family.

    I was also able to spend a few days with Cleaver, who now lived in New Jersey. It was so good seeing her. We spoke for hours. It was so good to be able to tell someone about how I was really feeling. We went out to buy ice cream at 2 o'clock in the morning. It was most unusual for me since the shops in the UK do not stay open that late. I felt comforted being around her. Our few days flew by so quickly. I

Forgiveness: The Journey to Healing the Heart

truly wanted to stay with Cleaver for much longer, but my plans had been set. Sadly I left my sister-friend.

After my trip to New York, I took the Greyhound bus back to Canada. It was nice being back with my big sister Gen. I loved that connected feeling I got when I was with her. When I was supposed to return to the UK, I extended my ticket for another two weeks. The truth was that I really did not want to go home to Keith. I missed my children so much. If they were in Canada with me, I would never have come back to the UK.

I eventually headed home to the UK. Nothing much had changed in my home life while I had been gone, but I was happy to be back for my children's sake. There was a convention being held in our Bishop's church in London. It was a great convention. The main speaker, Bishop Wagner, had come from our sister church in America. He was preaching and teaching. He spoke on a biblical topic and then asked the congregation if we agreed with his viewpoint. If we did, he asked us to stand up. I stood up, and a few others from our church stood as well. I could see Pastor Woods glaring at those of us who had dared to stand up. I saw the fire in his eyes, even if no one else could.

After the convention, we were back in Birmingham and Pastor Woods decided not to have Sunday service. He told the choir to de-robe because he was going to teach Bible school that day instead. He proceeded to get the board out and teach us what he thought we should know. I listened, but I was bored of listening to him. He was trying to force us to see the Bible from his point of view and was angry

Audreia Josephs

with us for standing up in London. Lots of people had agreed with Bishop Wagner, but they now sat cowering with no voice. Evangelist Powell, an elder who had been in the church since she was a young girl, bravely stood up to make a point and was told to sit down. I felt and saw the disrespect in that ego-centred behaviour. I decided that I too would speak up since so few of the others would. I stood up and raised a point. Pastor Woods called me stupid and told me to also sit down. I sat and decided that this would be the last time that I would ever come back to this church. Instead I started staying home with my children. We found other fun things to do instead of attending services. Keith was not amused with me, but he could not do anything about it.

Howard, Mark and Mavis still came and visited me. One week Mavis and Mark had told me that they were coming to visit me on Saturday. I had gone shopping to buy the food that I would prepare for our meal, and I came back home to a mess. The children were running around the house that I had cleaned up. The kitchen sink was full of dirty dishes, and Keith sat in his usual spot watching TV. I was angry, but I took it in and started to clean up the house. I washed, cooked and cleaned, all the time cussing under my breath. Keith watched TV all through this. He did not even offer to help me. Mavis and Mark arrived. I put my best face on. I did not want my new young brother and sister to see how distressed I was. I kept smiling and made out that everything was alright. I seated Mark, Mavis and the children around the dining table, and I gave everyone their food. I dished up Keith's

Forgiveness: The Journey to Healing the Heart

food. He was still sat in the same place that he had been sitting all day. I walked towards him with his plate of food in my hand. He stretched out his hands for the plate. I thought how he dare stretch out his hand for something that he had not helped me with at all. I was so tired. Something snapped in my head. I remembered my mother carrying the tray of food up the stairs to my step-father, and I remembered my promise to myself. I lost it. I lost my last piece of sanity. I pushed the plate of food in Keith's face and turned to walk away. Keith got up and grabbed me. I slapped him in his face, and a fight broke out between us. I had forgotten that my brother and sister Mark and Mavis were there in the next room with my children. I had forgotten everything. I only remembered when my brother Mark held me, trying to hold me back from ripping Keith to shreds. My children were crying. It was one hell of a commotion. I told Keith that now his mother can finally have a real reason to dislike me. I could see the shock on both my brother's and my sister's faces. I tried to comfort my children. There was nothing else I could do except feel ashamed that I had allowed myself to get to that point. I was ashamed that my children, brother and sister had seen me as a raging woman. I knew that the whole church was going to hear about this.

Keith could not go to church the next day. I had ripped up his face with my nails pretty badly. When his brother Tom saw his face, he was in shock that I could have done so much damage to his brother. Every time someone came to visit us and saw the state of Keith's face, I felt ashamed all over again. Pastor Woods heard about the fight, and

Audreia Josephs

he wanted us both to come to church to discuss it. I thought, 'The whole lot of them lying, back-stabbing people can kiss my ass.' Keith could dance to Pastor Woods tune on his own.

Forgiveness: The Journey to Healing the Heart

CHAPTER 13
Loss

I was still working for the agency. They had sent me to the air cargo centre, and I was now working for Fedex doing imports. The day that I started work, another young lady named Primrose started that afternoon. Strangely enough, Primrose had also been in the church and left, so we had something in common. Primrose was also a singer. She had song backing vocals with a few local bands. Fedex was new both in Birmingham and to the air cargo centre. They needed a lot of staff. The agency was supplying the staff, and through them I met Jennifer, June, Amanda, Monica, Andy, Belinda and Giles. These people would become more like family than friends to me. After a short time at Fedex, we were all hired permanently. Now with more job security, I was able to find somewhere for my children and me to live. I found a housing association that offered me a beautiful, newly-built three bedroom house. Ironically the house was 200 yards from where had gotten my first job with Keith. I could see the factory from my bedroom. When I told Keith that I was taking the children and leaving him, he went out and bought me flowers and chocolates. I told him that it was too little too late. After all the years of being with him, he had hardly ever bought me a birthday, Christmas or anniversary gift. He always forgot my birthday or our anniversary. Now here he was trying to buy me with flowers and chocolates. I told him that I was not that cheap, and it was too little, too late.

    I did not have any furniture for the new house yet, but I started packing the children's clothes. When Keith realised that I really was leaving, he cried and pleaded for me not to go or take the children. When he saw that I was intent on going, he started pulling on Stephen's arm. I pulled Stephen back to me. Keith continued to pull Stephen. I had to stop. Our child was not a tug of war. Keith went to the front door and blocked it. All the children were now crying. I told Keith that I wasn't leaving without my children. He told me that they were his children as well. He kept saying that they were all he had. He said that their schools and life were here. We continued like this for what seemed like hours. In the end, I gave up. The children were tired, so I put them to bed. I had no intention of spending another night in that house with him, so I left on my own. I told Keith to meet me the next day at Pizza Hut with the children.

    I left the house in a state of shock. I had had no idea that I was going to leave without my children. I'm not sure how I got to my new home. I opened the door. There was nothing there except a microwave that I had bought. In the lounge there was a red mattress from a captain's bed that I had bought second-hand from a friend. I sat in that lounge and stared at the ceiling all night until it was time to go to

Forgiveness: The Journey to Healing the Heart

work.

I went to work as usual and painted on a happy face. Inside I was hurting. After work I met Keith and the children at Pizza Hut. The children were fine. They held a competition to see who could eat the most pizza. Peter shouted, 'I've eaten nine pieces.' They had no idea that their father and I were discussing them and where they would live. Keith and I agreed that the children would live with him. I went back home with them, put them to bed, kissed them and left. It was so hard putting them to bed and leaving.

In the first few days after leaving, I thought about going back to Keith just so that my children would have the both of us together. I spoke to my mum about it. I told her how I was feeling about all of it. She reminded me how close Keith and I lived to the mental institution. Highcroft Mental Institution had been only 200 yards away from our home. She said that if I just kept on trying to keep up appearances, I would end up in there, unaware even that that my children were only 200 yards away from me. I gave our conversation some serious thought.

The one thought that kept me from going insane was that they were with their father. He had always been a very good father. They would spend weekends and school holidays with me. I would come and put them to bed every evening. I would buy anything that they needed. I couldn't take them away from their home and place them in my empty home. I left them smiling, but inside I felt sick. I felt that I

Audreia Josephs

was being punished for past judgement.

A few years earlier, a friend had split up with her husband and had left her children with him. I had judged her unfairly. I had said, 'How could she leave her children? She should have left the man and taken her children.' I had no idea what the dynamics of that relationship were. I had stood outside looking in. Now I knew that I was going to be judged in the same way. I felt that I had brought it upon myself, me and my big, uninformed, judgmental mouth.

What I have learnt from that experience is that people will read the headlines of your life but won't know the full story. To this day some people still have a judgmental attitude towards me because of what happened back then. I now choose not to give my power away to that feeling.

I had amazing neighbours. On my left was Cynthia, who, I later found out from my father, was a distant relative. Cynthia had a daughter and a son. On my right lived Patsey and her two children. It was so good living next to those two women. They had no idea how down I felt on a daily basis. In fact I never told anyone about the deepest happenings in my mind. Whenever anyone saw me out or at work, I was still able to offer a smile, a kind word or a joke.

Whenever the boys came to spend a weekend with me, I always made sure that it was fun. It was also good that most of the people on that road had younger children, so my children always had someone to play with.

Forgiveness: The Journey to Healing the Heart

I always felt guilty for not being with my sons. I would spend lots of money on them. They had no idea how much I spent, and I never told them. Meanwhile the judgement that followed me was often unbearable. One day while walking through town, I bumped into George, Keith's father's uncle. I thought that he was going judge me as everyone else felt they could freely do to me. However he said that people break up every day and that he was not judging me. I felt so relieved. He told me that Doris had never liked me because I did not have a top job. I said to him, 'How could I have had a top job at the age of sixteen? Plus I had met her son at the same company. In fact he was there before me, and it was not a top job.' He said a few more things about Doris. I thanked George for letting me know. At least I wasn't going mad. I had always known, but it was good to have it confirmed.

Peter's birthday neared, so I decided to give him a Baskin Robbins party. Some of his school friends were able to attend, but his guests mainly consisted of his cousins. They enjoyed themselves so much. I took lots of pictures. I had no idea that these pictures would become my only comfort when I was unable to see my sons.
At first everything seemed to be working well with Keith and my arrangement, but then it changed. At first Keith insisted that the children go to church with him on Sunday. That meant that I would only have them for Saturday. Then one day the boys said that they had started going to football, so that was the end of my Saturdays. By Christmas my home was furnished, and the boys' room was ready

for them. I had bought all kinds of food and was waiting for them to arrive. I excitedly went to the door when I heard the knock. There stood my three sons. They came in. 'Where's your bags?' I said to them. 'Dad said that we can't stay.' 'What do you mean you can't stay?' I said to them. 'Dad said that we have to go to gran's.' I went outside to the car where their father still sat. I shouted, 'What do you mean the boys are not staying?' 'You know mom has the family over for Christmas, and she wants all of us there,' he said. I saw in Keith's eyes that he was enjoying this. He held the power. I also felt that his mother had been behind this. This would not be the last time that Keith would do this.

After splitting up with Keith, people who I had known me throughout my life commented on how well I looked, saying that I had looked like an old woman when I was in the church.
One day my brother Howard came to visit me. He was attending church, though it was a different church. He had gotten engaged to a young lady called Pam. He told me that I should go back to my husband. I told him that he did not know what he was talking about and that when he had lived some real life he could come back and speak to me on this subject.

I wanted to get divorced from Keith, but I did not have the marriage certificate. That had been left behind along with all the wedding pictures. I went to the registry office. I told them that I would like a copy of my marriage license. They gave me a form to fill out. I put all the details on it. We had been married on 1st May 1982. The office staff looked in the file for the 1st of May and came back saying

Forgiveness: The Journey to Healing the Heart

that they could not find any documents for that date with my name on it. Was I sure I had been married on that date? Now I was confused. I knew that date clearly because I had chosen it. I asked them to look again. They took a very long time to get back to me. The woman in the registry office told me that I must have got my dates mixed up because they had found it in the file for the 11th of May. I insisted that I had been married on the 1st of May. She said that they would have to bring in the police if I was right. I stopped her and said that I might have gotten the dates wrong. I later checked the 11th of May 1982; it was a Tuesday. No one in our church would have been married on a Tuesday. I knew what Pastor Woods had done. He had falsified the marriage licenses. After a marriage, it must be registered within seven days. The church had a wedding every week, and Pastor Woods brought all the licenses to the registry office in batches. He would have added an extra number 1 to it so that everything fit date-wise. I am sure that he never thought that anyone would ever find out. But by falsifying this official document, he had made the marriage null and void, meaning that I was not really, officially married. I could have said something and allowed the police to go to the church and investigate it, but I chose not to. If the pastor had done this with our marriage license, how many others would he have done the same thing to? For me this was further confirmation that that church was not the place for me.

  I saw my solicitor who told me that I could not get divorced for five years because of a lack of grounds. I changed my name to Audreia

Audreia Josephs

Haughton by deed poll. I did it on purpose. My father had once told me that girls give their fathers' names away, but I had never been given my father's name. I really wanted to let him know how wrong he was.

Mothers' Day came. I knew that the church normally gave out flowers to the children to give to their mothers. When I went to visit my sons, they told me that their father had made them go up and get the flowers, and had told them to give the flowers to Doris, their grandmother. I was hurt. She had not given birth to them, and she was not their mother. This sort of behaviour continued for years. I felt like I was a surrogate. Whenever I saw any of the church people around, they would look down their nose at me. I had only a few true friends in that church.

One day I bumped into Nathan's godmother Kim. I had not seen her since I had left Keith, and she told me off. She said that I had not given Keith a chance. I was upset and asked if that was really what she thought. She knew about what had been going on in my life. I had told her some of it, and she knew about how badly Keith's mother had treated me. I thought that if she could think that about me, then I did not stand a hope in hell with other people who knew nothing about my life. I began to realise that the people that I had surrounded myself with when I had tried to banish the dark feeling in church meetings could be the most judgmental of all.

When my children were on their six week school holidays, I was working and therefore unable to have them during the week. Keith

Forgiveness: The Journey to Healing the Heart

was now working and had arranged for the boys to stay with Kim and Grace. I had found out from someone else that my sons were staying there. I had the day off work to attend the dentist. After I had finished at the dentist, I went over to Kim's house so that I would be able to see my sons. I rang the bell. At first I could see everyone in the house through the window. I rang the bell again when no one came to the door. Still no one came to open the door. I rang the doorbell again. This time Kim opened the door. She told me that I could not see my children. She said that Keith had left them with her, and that they were her responsibility. I was in shock. I never thought that someone whom I had chosen to be my son's godmother would block me from seeing my own children. I wanted to cry on the spot. I told her thank you for looking after my children and turned around and left. I walked up the road crying. People commit murder and were treated better. The church had a moral duty to Keith. I was the big sinner and should be beaten at every turn. I had become the scourge of society.

    I had met Eddie through a group of shared friends. Eddie knew about the whole drama, and he would sometimes take me out for dinner or lunch. Some of the bitter and twisted people in the church kept making up stories about me. Keith kept repeating all the stories that people told him. One day I was walking on the street when I heard a car horn blowing. I turned around and looked in the direction from where the sound had come. It was Pastor Woods. He beckoned for me to come over to him. I thought, 'Shit. He knows it's me. I can't act like

Audreia Josephs

I haven't seen him. I'm not in the mood for this right now.' He said, 'Praise the Lord, Sister Audrey. How are you?' 'Fine,' I said. 'We have missed you at church. I have been looking out for you for some time. Please come in the car so that we can talk.' As you know, I have been brought up to respect my seniors, so I thought that I would show him some common courtesy. I got into his car, and he parked it. 'Sister, I hear that you have a boyfriend. You have been seen out with a man. God will charge you on the last day.' I said to Pastor Woods, 'With the greatest of respects, let me get out of your car before I say the wrong thing to you.' With that, I stepped out of his car and went about my business.

Eddie had been working as a delivery man. He had a dream of setting up a business of his own. I told him that he could work out of my home. I was still working for Fedex at the airport and loving it. I had never earned so much money. Primrose and I had seemed to become firm friends. I was also making all kinds of celebration cakes for customers. Eddie had big dreams. One of his dreams was to buy a house in Florida. He bought all the magazines that he could find. One day my mum and some of the family came to visit me at home, and mum saw the Florida magazines. She asked if she could take some home with her. I said yes. A few weeks later my mum said that she wanted to leave the UK. She wanted to sell her UK house and buy one in Florida. I told her that she should take a holiday there to see how she felt. She had a cousin who was living there. I bought her a ticket

Forgiveness: The Journey to Healing the Heart

with my Fedex staff discount.

Before any of us could take a second thought, mum called to say that she had found the house of her dreams. It was a four bedroom house with a swimming pool. My mum and John 'Nekep' had split up some years ago. When they had first split up, John 'Neckep' lived downstairs and my mum lived upstairs. It had taken them five years to come to an amicable arrangement with regards to the house. John 'Neckep' had now moved out of Whitehall Road and had brought another house on Holiday Road. I guess my mum must have felt that the time for change had come. The speed with which everything started changing for her was shocking for us. Mum found a buyer for Whitehall Road, sold and gave away the items that she no longer needed and packed everything else in barrels to be shipped over to the States.

Life also got better for Eddie, and our friendship just naturally fell into a relationship. His mortgage broker business had taken off in a big way, and he was now able to leave his delivery job. His attitude changed. I could always tell if he was on the telephone to a female client. He would be laughing at the top of his voice and flirting.

My 30th birthday was coming up, and I wanted to go to Hawaii. I had seen it on a TV programme called Wish You Were Here. I was able to secure a discount for Eddie and myself to go. We flew thirteen long hours from the UK to Los Angeles, waited for four hours and then took another six hour flight. It was really nice being in Hawaii, but I became

Audreia Josephs

aware that I had come with the wrong person. Eddie had started putting me down in little ways, and I wished that I had never brought him with me. When we got back to the UK, I knew that things had changed between us. Eddie was my now, but he wouldn't be my future. I needed to find my own future.

Forgiveness: The Journey to Healing the Heart

CHAPTER 14
Betrayal

I was still in contact with my brother Jim in America, but Jim would play games with me. He would call me and have a whole conversation with me before he told me that it was a three-way call with our father on the other line. I hated America for being able to have three-way calls; we did not have that facility in the UK at the time. I loved my brother, but I hated his games. I would hear my father say, 'Hello.' Jim knew that I was not interested in having a conversation with my father, and he was trying to be the peacemaker. I was finding it hard to have a light-hearted conversation with Jim just in case I said something personal and my father was listening. At the start of our phone conversations, I would ask Jim if this was a three-way call. If it was, I would hang up. 'You're not tricking me into speaking to Dad.' I could tell when dad was listening most of the time, so I knew that he would have heard what I said. I also knew that Jim and dad were very close and that they spent a lot of time together. 'Why do you have to be like that?' Jim would say. I would reply 'Maybe it's because Dad has not done shit for me.' Jim continued to do this for many years. He never gave up trying to get me to speak to our father. But Jim also knew that he had to be careful when it came to conversations about Dad with me. He also didn't know me that well. We grew up on two different continents.

    I was still working for Fedex. I would call my brother Jim from time to time. One day Jim asked me if I had any beautiful UK friends. As I was sitting next to Primrose, I handed the phone to her. Primrose and Jim struck up a conversation. She was telling him that her family came from Portland in Jamaica, which was the same place where our family came from. My father must have been with Jim. He overheard the conversation and asked if he could speak to the young lady. My father started asking Primrose a whole load of questions, and before long we realised that there was a family connection.

    I was still getting to spend the odd weekend with my sons. One day while they were at my house, I walked past their bedroom, stopped and listened. I knew that I should not be snooping on my sons, but somehow I still found myself listening. Stephen was saying, 'Who does she think she is telling us what to do?' Nathan followed with, 'Yeah, she always tells us what to do.' Peter agreed. I was shocked. I just stood there. It hurt like a knife through my heart. I took everything personally when it came to those three boys. I opened the door, and all three of them jumped. I told them that I had heard what they had said, and I asked if that was what they really thought about me. It wasn't so much the words that they had said that had hurt. It was more the sentiment behind the words. I left the room and never mentioned

Forgiveness: The Journey to Healing the Heart

it again. I had given my three sons the power to hurt me, more than anyone else could, because I had thought that I deserved it.

My brother Howard set a wedding date and was getting married soon. Jim called me. He said that our father wanted to come back to the UK for Howard's wedding. Our father had burnt bridges with Howard's mother and had nowhere to stay. I said to Jim, 'What does that have to do with me?' Jim said, 'Audrey, please, he's our father. Let him stay at your house.' I swear if this was not my brother speaking to me, I would have gone off like a firework. I was thinking, 'What the ****! Is he really asking me if our father could stay in my house?' I said to him, 'You must be mad to be asking me that.' Jim tried again, and again, and again. I had more respect for my brother than I had for our father. Jim wore me down, and I ended up saying yes. For days I was cussing myself for saying yes to Jim. I didn't really want my father in my house, enjoying what I had worked hard for and with no contribution. I sure did not want to cook and clean any thing for him. The day he arrived, Eddie and I went and picked him up. I was just about able to say hi to my father. It felt strange being in the same space as him. I tried my best to look and feel normal around him. We got to my house, and I showed him to his room. I gave him the food that I had prepared earlier. He seemed grateful. It was strange watching TV and trying to make conversation with him. I didn't know what to say. I was grateful for Eddie's presence. He made a lot of small talk with my father. He didn't have the same history as my father and I had, so it was easier for

Audreia Josephs

him.

    The next day Keith dropped the boys off. They were happy to see their granddad again. They had been much younger the last time they had seen him. My boys were growing into to handsome young boys. One of them even had the cheek to look like my father. Good thing that I thought that my daddy was a handsome man. Strong DNA. No matter what was going on in my life, I always wanted my sons to know that I loved them and would be there for them. I attended all three of my sons' parent evenings and sports days. I was the big mouth Mom cheering my boys on from the sidelines. I understood the school system better than their father and was able to challenge them if needs be. No one was going to take advantage of any of my sons. All three of my sons attended different schools. Stephen and Nathan's school were miles out of town. I had to take a bus for miles, and then walk for miles before I got to the schools. Their father never attended any of their school meetings. I wanted my sons to feel supported.

    The day of Howard's wedding arrived. Peter was a pageboy, and I had given Keith money to buy Stephen and Nathan new suits. However he had decided not to buy them. I did not know this until the day of the wedding. I was upset. Keith had sent them to the wedding with mismatched clothing. All I could do was not let them see me getting upset and try to enjoy the day with them. Quality time with them was becoming more and more rare, but we all enjoyed our family time together at Howard's wedding.

Forgiveness: The Journey to Healing the Heart

A few days after the wedding, my father said that he would like to visit a few friends. He had made arrangements with Eddie, and he asked me to come along with them. The first place my father wanted to go to was a house in the Aston area of Birmingham. Dad got out of the car and went into this house. Eddie and I stayed in the car. I did not know to whom the house belonged, but a little while later; my father came out of the house with some young men. He made a kind of introduction. He said to me, 'You see these young men? I brought them up like my sons.' Now though this house was about less than hundred yards from the church that I had attended for the past eight years, I don't ever remember seeing those people before. Why was my father telling me that he helped to bring up someone else's children, not just one, but a whole group of young men, in an area that he had not lived in? 'WHAT DID YOU JUST SAY TO ME? Did you just say that you brought up these boys as your sons?' I let him say his good-byes, and I did not speak for a whole minute, maybe two. I think that my father must have realised what he had said to me. 'You should be ashamed of yourself, saying that to me,' I said to my father. Eddie told me, 'Don't speak to your father like that.' 'Shut up,' I told him. 'And keep out of this.' I spoke with such fire that I even surprised myself. I went back to my father. 'How dare you tell me that you brought up those boys, when you did nothing for me? Are those young men your sons?' I asked him. He said no. I said, 'You would say that. So when did you come to Birmingham to bring these boys up?' I spat. 'No, no,' my

Audreia Josephs

father said. 'Their farad is ah fren. Dem boy born ah Wolverhampton.' I wanted to kick my father out of the car. In fact I wanted to get him out of my house as soon as I could. I stopped speaking. I felt my blood boiling, and if I had said another word it was not going to be pretty. My father pretty much kept out of my way for the next few days. It was almost time for him to leave, and I was glad. I had had enough of his life's surprises.

 I had been working for Fedex for a few years when we first heard whispers about the company relocating. Suddenly, bang, there it was on the TV. We were being made redundant. We just stared at each other. For the next few weeks we felt as if we were working in a morgue. After being made redundant, I went back to the agency. I continued getting a steady work, but I did not want to do any more chef work. I had acquired too many burns on my arms over the years. You also couldn't have long nails as a chef, and my nails had considerably grown over the last few years.

 Eddie's business meanwhile was doing really well. He now rented office space, and he decided that he now wanted to own property. He had done a few mortgage deals and knew how the game worked. He bought a property in my name, which he then rented out to others and took the equity - the excess money that the property was worth. He used these to buy properties in other people's names and did the same thing with those properties. He paid the people for using their names, though to this day I have never been paid for my part.

Forgiveness: The Journey to Healing the Heart

Finally he bought property in his own name using the equity that he had gathered from the other properties. I never noticed the game he was playing at the time. He never put it the property in our name, though we chose everything together. We went to auctions together. I made curtains. I got my friends, who were furniture makers, to make handmade bedroom furniture. We chose carpets. I stripped off old wallpaper and redecorated. We did everything together, to the point that I damaged my back.

But something spoke to me and told me to keep hold of my house.

Eddie was now starting to make some real good money. He was paying for most everything. We went to top restaurants and drank expensive wines. He took to calling me Miss Frumps, meaning walk behind him. He would say, 'You're attractive, but you're not pretty.' All of this was working on the insecure me. He flirted with other women in front of my face and didn't care that I saw. One day he came to my house wearing a T-shirt that he refused to take off. I started making a fuss about why he didn't want to show me his back. In the end he must have had enough, and he took off the T-shirt. He had fingernail scratches all over his back. He tried to tell me that he had owed money to someone, and they had roughed him up, but I did not believe him. I knew that he was lying. I got in to the whole drama face with him. He still tried to convince me. He slept on the sofa.

In 1992 I had a burning desire to become a counsellor. I felt that

Audreia Josephs

I would be good at it. I got the university prospectus and arranged to find out what my options were. I wanted to start a basic counselling course. I was so nervous. When I got to the University of Central England for my interview, my interviewer told me that I was an advanced student and that I should consider enrolling on the advanced course. I was in shock; I had never thought of myself as advanced in anything. I had studied psychology a few years earlier with my friend Angela, but I had not been aware that I could use those credits towards this course. I was so excited. I had always gone past that university on the bus. I loved its look and had always wanted to study there. The university accepted my application to the course. The course was facilitated by an organisation called Values Education For Life. I was attending my course at my dream campus, the Faculty of Education on Westbourne Road, Edgbaston. I kept thinking that I was going show everybody that I was not stupid. A part of this course was that we were sent out on one day placement in a school. I was sent to Dudley High School. This is where I got my first taste of working with young people. A few months later, I was sent to Park View School as their Social Advisor. I wished my school teachers could see me now.

For New Years, I went to Yorkshire to ring in 1993. I stayed at an all-inclusive hotel, which put on a really nice New Year's event and meal. The only thing that spoilt it was that Eddie was there. We had been growing more and more distant from each other, and deep in my heart, I knew that this was going to be the last New Year we celebrated together.

Forgiveness: The Journey to Healing the Heart

I had always wanted to go to the historical town of Bath. Eddie had promised that he would take me one day, but it was just one of those places that we could never seem to get to. I said to Eddie as a joke that if we ever went to Bath, then I would know that we were over.

A few months later, here we were in the spa town of Bath. Neither of us had planned this day. We had gone out shopping and were in the car when we decided to go on an adventure. That was the side of him that I had really liked. 'Where do you want to go?' I jokingly said, 'Bath.' And off we went.

I was studying part-time and needed a job. My sister Jade was working in a call centre. She said that there were vacancies and that I should come for an interview. I was still working for the agency, but I wanted a permanent job. I went for an interview at the call centre and got the job. The job was basic, but it was okay. My coworkers were a friendly group of women. One of the women I met called Maria told me that her sister-in-law lived around the corner and that she sold designer clothes. A few of us were interested and went around to Maria's sister-in-law who was named Anna. Anna was a very beautiful petite woman, with long, beautifully flowing hair. Somehow I found myself thinking, 'She looks like Eddie's type.' I had no idea where that thought came from, but once it had entered my head, it stayed there. Anna was very friendly. She mentioned wanting to moved out of her apartment and buying a house. The conversation must have been divine timing for her, because I said to her that my partner helps people to get mortgages. Pen in hand, I gave her his number.

When I got home, I told Eddie about my day. I told him that I had met the woman of his dreams. I told him that she looked a bit like Diana Ross and that she was his type. He brushed off what I was saying as a joke. I told him that Anna wanted help in getting a mortgage and that she was going to call him. Sure enough, Anna called Eddie. I knew the day she called because I could hear the way he was flirting and carrying on. I said to him again that she was his type. I knew I wasn't his type, based purely on how he spoke to and treated me. I felt the opposite of me was Anna.

Anna and Eddie's meeting was set. I knew the day of the meeting, and where it would take place. Eddie tried to assure me that what I was saying about Anna was all in my head and that we were fine. When I got home, I asked him what he had thought of Anna. He tried to pass it off as still in my mind, but I could see it in his eyes. I knew that they had connected.

I told Anna's sister-in-law Maria what I had felt. She told me that Anna had a partner.
Eddie gained a spring in his step. He was not aware that I could see the changes in him. We moved into the new house. I should have been feeling happy, but somehow I felt like an uninvited guest.
I wanted to buy some more clothes from Anna. I went around to her house. I bought some more clothes. I told her what I had felt in regard

to her and Eddie. She said that she knew that we were together and that she would never do that to me. Not long after we had moved into the new house, Eddie said that we should take a break. 'A break?' I thought. 'Why?'

I was so glad that I had kept my house. I moved my things and myself back into my house. One day one of my friends called me to say that she had seen Eddie at a graduation ceremony. She was there because her sister had been graduating. She had seen Eddie and had walked over to him and enquired where I was. Eddie had been lost for words. She then noticed that he was with someone else. When she described the woman that had been with Eddie, I knew that it had been Anna. A few days later I bumped into an old friend who I had not seen for some time who told me that she had seen Eddie at the cinema with a woman.

    I had not seen Eddie for a few weeks. There was some mail for him at my house, so I decided that I would drop it off to him in the morning. I got up early and took the bus to Eddie's house. I no longer considered it our house. As I approached the house, I heard laughing. I walked faster towards the house. I saw them before they saw me. Eddie and Anna were coming out of the house. They looked up and saw me. I walked up to Eddie and said, 'Here's your mail.' He looked at me and said that he and Anna were doing some business together. I replied, 'Is that what you're calling it now?' I was in stunned silence. Eddie escorted Anna to the car first before he got in and drove off. I just stood there like a fool. I had handed him over to Anna on a plate.

Audreia Josephs

Eddie came to visit me and told me that we were over and that he thought he only had to click his fingers if he wanted me back. Wow. I really did not mean anything to him.
I felt like this was my punishment for all of my past wrongs. It hurt to see how right I had been about Eddie and Anna. But even still, I had not seen the last of Eddie.

After this my head just went into free flow. Unable to eat or sleep, I lost all and all concentration. I had tried so hard always to move on, to find positivity, and to be better, but here I was without anything, without even myself. Here I was in my dream university, working towards my dream career, and I could not focus.

For a long time, my sons were my only sunshine on the horizon. They were my greatest teachers in the art of self-forgiveness. When they were around, I came out of my insane mode. As soon as they left, I fell straight back into it.

Love and forgiveness were also my teachers. I was being carved, shaped and moulded.
On New Year's day in 1994, I sat listening to Toni Braxton's 'Breathe Again'. My life would soon kick into another high level of drama, which would involve love, disappointment, prison and meeting royalty. My biggest life lessons were even still yet to happen. But life had already taught me so many things. Though it has many twists and turns, life is best experienced with many friends and much forgiveness.

Forgiveness: The Journey to Healing the Heart

Epilogue

If someone had told me that I would ever write a book - let alone write it in seven weeks - I would have told them that they were mad.

I sat down in front of my laptop, thinking, 'How do I start writing a book? What do I have to say?' 'Start with you,' my inner voice said. I had always had stories somewhere deep down inside of me. I had said them out loud over the past 20 years. My life stories wanted to be born. As soon as I put my fingers to the keys, the stories jumped out. They all want to be heard. They were fighting to get out. They did not even want to come out in order. As soon as I started writing one story, another one would try to jump out. Things I thought I had long forgotten and stories I didn't remember until they stood up and asked for their time to be heard. I saw people and pictures in my head.

It's amazing how divine timing works. When the student is ready, the teacher will appear.

I was challenged to write this book. I rose to the challenge. I had had no idea when I started writing this book that it would give me cause for the deepest personal introspection that I have ever done.

I had been coaching and speaking about the art of forgiveness for some time. Here I was thinking that I had covered every aspect of my own forgiveness issues. I thought that I had forgiven everything and everybody in my life. I had done the prayers, meditations, affirmations and mantras. I had read the books, done the courses and watched the videos.

This book made me realise that I was not being completely true with myself. While writing this book, I sometimes found myself so angry. At times I shook so much that I thought that I would never stop shaking. I would have to lay on the ground and meditate until I found my peace again. I had to tell all the lies that tried to stand in front of me that they were illusions. My mantra had to be, 'Anything that is not love is an illusion.' I had to keep saying that over and over again as I wrote this book.

I knew that forgiveness was a choice.

One day my husband asked me how I dealt with writing about the difficult issues. I told him that I was detached. I wrote as if I was an observer, a third person writing about my life. That was how I approached it. That worked for some aspects of this book, but there also came a time when I knew there were going to be real emotions in these pages.

I did not know that writing would make me feel so exposed. At times I felt naked.

Writing this book has been a gift. It has enabled me to shine a light on the dark areas of my inner self and the parts that I had refused

Forgiveness: The Journey to Healing the Heart

or forgotten to look at.

I am aware that I was too young to deal with some of the things that have happened to me. Now as an adult, I could revisit them with the healing tools that I now have.

I have seen how I have been protected and preserved by my Creator. It has caused me to have more gratitude. It has caused me to love more, both myself and others. I have learnt to trust my vision and inner feelings. It has made me see that I am not who I thought I was. It has made me see how strong and resilient I am.

This book has caused me to celebrate me.

Up until recently, I had thought that if you said that you forgive, that it would cover every issue that you had ever had in your life. Going through this process has shown me that one size does not fit all.

Forgiveness is awareness. If you are not aware of an issue, how can you forgive it?

I thought that some of my hard exterior was my personality. I had no idea that it was an issue that I had with a lack of forgiveness. I had tried to protect myself since I was a child. I had not been aware that my internal protection had become a part of my external personality.

That lack of awareness caused bumps in my life's road.

Writing this book has become therapy for me. It has become valuable learning for me.

Throughout writing this book, my fears also spoke to me. What if you

Audreia Josephs

make your family and friend mad? What if people laugh at you? What if nobody is interested in your book? You are naked and exposed.
I had to address those voices of fear.

Firstly, to my fear of the anger of family and friends: This book is about my journey. If you have happened to cross my path on my life journey, then you may well be in this book. I have not written this book from a bitter perspective. Perhaps if I had written this five years ago, it might have been a bitter perspective. But I have written it now, and it is not.

Secondly, to my fear of laughter: I love laughing, and laughing has helped to carry me through some of the hardest things that I have ever been through. I have been laughed at. I have laughed with many people. Most people who know me know that I am a person who loves a good laugh. Laughter is good, so good in fact that there is a therapy called 'laughter therapy'. I no longer have a fear of people laughing at me.

I have stripped and exposed myself, in the hope that healing can take place, without wearing the cloak of shame.

And my loudest reply to fear is this: ANYTHING THAT IS NOT LOVE IS AN ILLUSION.

Forgiveness is a two-way street. As I forgive all for past hurts and preserved hurts, I also ask for forgiveness.

I ask the beautiful souls that chose me as their mother, Stephen, Nathan and Peter, to forgive me. I know that they got caught up in

Forgiveness: The Journey to Healing the Heart

my hurt, fear and confusion. I am grateful that they chose me as their mother. They have taught me so much about myself.

I forgive my mother. A hurt girl trying to survive in a world of pain and rejection. Seeking love. Giving her power away to men.

I am now a woman, and can see the world from her perspective. Since I have been writing this book. I have had occasion to speak to my mother about why she treated me so badly in the past. She was not really able to explain to me why. She did, however, apologise to me.

At first when she apologised to me, it did not feel like how I thought it would feel. I had waited for almost 50 years for it, and now here it was. I was not sure what I had expected, but it didn't erase it. I was still mad and upset about how she had treated me.

I had to go deep down inside of myself. I could not understand why I was so mad, especially about something that I had considered forgiven. Then I realised that I had forgiven her for some things but not others. This was a revelation to me.

I had wanted to hold on to the pain and conversation, of the damage that she had caused. I wanted to be the one who could now issue the beatings to her with my words. Somewhere in my mind I was wearing the badge of pain with pride.

Now the time has come to put them all down. Detach and dissolve.

This book has caused me to revisit places that I had not been to for many years. It has caused me to seek out the people who cared and

Audreia Josephs

loved me, just because. People like Ivy Drysdale.

Since writing this book, I have reconnected with the Drysdale family. Things have dramatically changed in Ivy's life, and I felt sad that I had not stayed in touch. I am grateful that she is still here with us and that I have access to seeing her.

Glenda (Grace) and Violet (Kim): I have also had occasion to reconnect with Violet. We made our peace with each other. Glenda and I never really reconnected. She remained in the church, and she kept a wall between herself and me. We did speak, but we were never comfortable in each other's space. We didn't see eye-to-eye on matters that were important to both of us. Every time I saw her, she would invite me back to church. She saw me as a backslider, and there was nothing I could do to change her point of view. Glenda passed away in 2012. It hurt knowing that she had passed away and that we had not made up. I still loved her as my sister.

I will forever be grateful to Violet, her beautiful daughter Katrina - who my sons consider their big sister - and Glenda Phipps. I will never forget all the good these women did for my children and me. As for my Auntie Cassilda (Cassie) Clarke, her murder is still a very sensitive issue. The wounds of this loss continue to reverberate in our family, especially for her seven children. The pain is still there 40 years later.

I have had times that I have been lost in sadness and pain. All I could do was speak silent whispers to my Auntie Cassie.

I want Auntie Cassilda's children to know that she touched my

Forgiveness: The Journey to Healing the Heart

life in a very profound way and I honour her.

As for Maureen Vernon, with whom I was friends since we were both young girls, she helped me get through the trials that I had in my life. I could not have thought of a better person to have shared my adventures with. Always laughter, even when we both knew that there was pain. I am grateful that the Creator put you in my path.

To Edris Henry, I admire you. You are an amazing woman. My eldest son Stephen, who also happens to be your godson, is still alive because of your early teachings. I did not have a clue of how to care for a baby. Every day you supported me and encouraged me with no form of judgement. I am grateful for your fast-track lessons. I am so proud that you chose me to be your daughter Rebecca's godmother. Girl, you have taught me not to only have a vision but how to manifest that vision in my life.

I would like to ask for Forgiveness from all of my godchildren and their parents. Some of my earlier godchildren have no idea who I am. I was chosen because these parents thought that I would add value in their children's life, but now, in most instances, I am only a name or picture. I would love to reconnect. But even if we don't, I send you all love and joy.

And finally, to Cleaver A Walker, you and I must have been twins in a past life. Even though we have been separated by an ocean for the past 32 years, our friendship is as strong as ever. Even when we lost touch, our angel through your Uncle Sid (R.I.P) reconnected us. Over the years our lives seemed to have mirrored each other in so many

Audreia Josephs

respects. Your phone calls are always divinely timed. It's amazing how in tune we are to each other. I love how alike we are. I have had many friends that have come and gone, but you and I together are just the same as we were when we met in 1977. I turn in to girl-mode when I am with you. I am so grateful to have you in my life.

Printed in Great Britain
by Amazon